ART AND SOUL

ABOUT THE AUTHOR

Bruce L. Moon is an artist and art therapist with extensive clinical, teaching and administrative experience. He is a registered and board certified art therapist who holds a doctorate in creative arts with specialization in art therapy. Bruce is the Director of the Graduate Art Therapy program at Mount Mary College in Milwaukee. His clinical practice of art therapy, focused on the treatment of emotionally disturbed children, adolescents, and adults, has spanned over twenty-seven years. He has lectured and led workshops at many universities in the United States and Canada.

Bruce is the author of *Existential Art Therapy: The Canvas Mirror, Essentials of Art Therapy Training and Practice, Introduction to Art Therapy: Faith in the Product, The Dynamics of Art As Therapy with Adolescents, Ethical Issues in Art Therapy, Working with Images: The Art of Art Therapists* and *Word Pictures: The Poetry and Art of Art Therapists.* He has also written a number of journal articles. Bruce brings to this project many years of experience in art studios, clinical settings, and educational institutions. His educational background is comprised of interdisciplinary training in theology, art therapy, education, and visual art. He is an active painter, songwriter, and performer.

Second Edition

ART AND SOUL
Reflections on an Artistic Psychology

By

BRUCE L. MOON, PH.D., ATR-BC

With a Foreword by
John Reece, Psy.D.

With a Preface by
Lynn Kapitan, Ph.D., ATR-BC

CHARLES C THOMAS • PUBLISHER, LTD.
Springfield • Illinois • U.S.A.

Published and Distributed Throughout the World by

CHARLES C THOMAS • PUBLISHER, LTD.
2600 South First Street
Springfield, Illinois 62704

©2004 by CHARLES C THOMAS • PUBLISHER, LTD.

ISBN 0-398-07523-9 (hard)
ISBN 0-398-07524-7 (paper)

Library of Congress Catalog Card Number: 2004048001

With THOMAS BOOKS *careful attention is given to all details of manufacturing
and design. It is the Publisher's desire to present books that are satisfactory as to their
physical qualities and artistic possibilities and appropriate for their particular use.*
THOMAS BOOKS *will be true to those laws of quality that assure a good name
and good will.*

Printed in the United States of America
GS-R-3

Library of Congress Cataloging-in-Publication Data

Moon, Bruce L.
   Art and soul : reflections on an artistic psychology / by Bruce L.
Moon ; with a foreword by John Reece ; with a preface by Lynn
Kapitan.--2nd ed.
      p. cm.
   Includes bibliographical references.
   ISBN 0-398-07523-9 (hbk.) -- ISBN 0-398-07524-7 (pbk.)
   1. Art therapy. 2. Soul. I. Title.

RC489 .A7M657 2004
616.89'1656--dc22
                                                      2004048001

FOREWORD

Clinical psychology has always included both art and science. In the past few decades, however, it seems to have focused far more closely on scientific understanding than upon its art. The de-emphasis of artistic psychology has left clinicians without access to key tools needed to deal with our clients' problems.

Scientific psychological inquiry provides useful, predictive knowledge of human behavior. Each day there are more discoveries about the complex interactions of the physical and the psychological realms, enabling clinical psychologists to be better prepared for battle with any number of disorders. To a scientifically-oriented clinician, a clinical problem can be reduced to understandable interactions of cognition, affect, and behavior by means of a careful and thorough cognitive/behavioral assessment. With that knowledge, the clinician researches the current literature to determine which intervention has shown the greatest amount of success in like cases. The intervention is applied, the behavioral results are carefully assessed, and then the therapist moves on to the next problem.

Behavioral assessment is reductionistic. Breaking a problem down to its component parts is the first aim of empiricism. However, an involvement of the client's *soul* in his or her psychological problems may frustrate a reductionistic inquiry. So many clinical syndromes submit successfully to the dissection of a behavioral assessment that it is perplexing to the scientist when such a dissection is disallowed by the vagaries of the soul. There is a stoppage in the flow of understandable, defined, reduced data. Often, the reason for the interruption of the information flow is unclear.

The empirical psychologist asks focused questions, answered in binary (yes/no), comparative (more or less discomfort), or digital (rate your anxiety on a scale from one to ten) formats. The scientist is on a quest for specific information, and the questions and observations are designed to produce measurable data. What the scientist is unable to work with is the absence of data. The question answered with a stony stare. The behavioral record sheet lost. A missed appointment. Pain expressed as a sigh instead of an integer.

Our scientist sifts through his data again, to attempt to find the cause of the data interruption. Nothing can be found in the cognitions, the affective patterns of the behavioral record to explain why there are now non-answers to vital questions.

The reason is soul. People are not simply cognitive/behavioral/affective automatons. The spirit of a person is not something that is constructed from the body alone. The personality doesn't own the soul. The body and the personality are there to support the willful, purposive aspect of the self. You cannot find the soul of a person in dissection of the personality any more than you can find the ideas you are now reading by tearing my computer apart.

The success of empirically based psychological treatment is that it is effective in dealing with problems that are not soul-based. Many affective/cognitive/behavioral knots can indeed be undone by reductionistic unraveling. In confronting such a problem, a clinician should offer the scientific solution to the human being that he or she faces. But caring clinicians should be prepared to understand that they might have come to a premature conclusion, based on an inquiry that is not complete. If the problem is soul-based, then a strictly empirical approach is inappropriate.

If my soul has been battered by a painful experience and I am questioning my life purpose, then it is not enough to simply show me the signs and symptoms of my "depressed" behavior to get me to change my cognitions and to medicate me. Such efforts may solve the problem, if you have defined the problem as the existence of "depressed behavior" and the solution as its absence. However, I may recreate my depression and take up its suffering all over again. There is a soul purpose in returning to the pain. The pain is there to be attended to, not deleted.

Many paths can approach soul, but science, acting alone isn't one of them. Soul defies empiricism, because there are no instruments that can measure it. Science is unequipped to analyze soul, to subject soul to prediction and control. What is needed is a greater understanding than our current psychological science can deliver unaided.

* * * * *

Science is unable to predict and control another class of powerful human phenomena: art. There are no scientific tests to measure aesthetic beauty absolutely, and none that can distinguish music from noise. Art is not containable by science, nor definable within it.

Art and soul are companions. Evidence abounds that art, in a vital way unlike science, can be *about* soul and a direct expression of it. The paintbrush, the guitar, the dancing body, the poet's quill are tools of the soul and can therefore be the tools of soul healing. Bruce Moon's life work has been to use those tools and to teach the use of those tools to others.

This book is a call to reintegrate the soul into treatment through art, a natural passageway. It is not a call to revolution, for psychology has not always been disconnected from soul and art.

Sigmund Freud and Carl Jung were patrons of art and recognized the integration of artistic images into psychological understanding. William James's empiricism eventually embraced soul and religious experience. However, during the ninety years or so since the prominence of these psychological pioneers, there has been a divorce from the soul. In current psychological thought, the ancestral patriarchs are the psychometrists Wundt and Tichener. Their carefully ordered laboratories are seen as the womb of our modern science. It is believed by some that psychology didn't exist before the age of psychometric measurement.

This is revisionist history. It ignores the constant thread of psychological investigation that stretches back in time to before history. There is no human mind that exists apart from humanness; therefore any exploration of humanness is a psychology. The prehistoric cave paintings document the freedom, willfulness, hopes, and triumphs of the earliest humans. They are paintings of soul. They are psychological.

A constant thread of psychology-as-humanness was broken in the twentieth century. Perhaps the divorce is symptomatic of a general un-souling of our culture, ourselves. But it need not be.

Science itself contains the essential elements of art, just as art embodies science. The two ways of knowing are not enemies, and are in fact two faces of the same human endeavors: to create understanding of our inner and outer worlds, and to communicate that understanding. Such endeavors are definitive of humanity; therefore the combined goal of art and science is to express humanness.

Art and science will someday be harmonious and not discordant. Robert Pirsig, among other thinkers, has already demonstrated the absurdity of the divorce. Nowhere is this absurdity more painfully enacted than in our current clinical psychology.

To attempt an art therapeutic approach with someone in a manic episode, without considering medication, is less than helpful. A "scientific" intervention, specifically a chemical treatment, has been shown to be effective in starting to return the manic person into a balanced state. In this state of improvement, help with the soul issues is possible. Similarly, it is neglectful to attempt to remove symptoms of anxiety without allowing the possibility that the person's fear is existential. You listen to the soul. If it needs a paintbrush to do its own healing work, you give it one.

Moon writes about "imagicide," the killing of images by analysis. Imagicide is misapplied science, a science against art. The soul produces an image which the scientist dissects, thereby killing it. This is one form of violence perpetrated by the split between artistic and scientific psychologies.

By means of a pun, I can illustrate a further harm of this divorce. If I pronounce the word as "image-aside," then I see the scientist simply pushing images away to one side, out of sight and out of mind. This is neglectful. Our clients will never stop making images for us because the soul demands that images be created. But I, the "scientific" psychologist, can endlessly push aside the images I am presented with. In so doing, I tell my client that his or her soul doesn't deserve my attention. It is superfluous and out of the question. This quiet violence is perhaps the most damaging of all.

* * * * *

The book in your hands is a book of reconciliation. It is a deeply generous book, in which artist Moon gives the gifts of artistic understanding to the clinicians who will accept them.

John Reece, Psy.D.
Westerville, Ohio

PREFACE

Several years ago, while in the midst of a struggle for finding balance between my personal and professional lives, I had a dream in which my friend and colleague Bruce Moon came to me and told me, "Wake up. You must get ready." Much as the reader will find here in *Art and Soul: Reflections on an Artistic Psychology,* the task at hand was a restoration of soul that would come about only through a waking up of my senses, a return to artistic consciousness from what had been a somnolent state, and an embrace of the artistic tradition of struggle. Yet he tells us not to fear, the "soul will be found wherever imaginative work is underway."

Waking up to the soul and vividness of artistic imagination can be an act of readiness to face with resilience the frightful instability around us in these times and in our particular culture. Rapid and profound changes in the community, family, and work structures also have been rippling through mental health care services in this country in recent years. Many therapists and their clients are left feeling fragmented and soulless, deprived of meaningful, healing relationships. Treatment processes have become increasingly superficial, mere time and sound bites of contact between client and therapist, thoroughly documented in fat files of assessments, medication records, and behavioral contracts for repeating, reoccurring hospitalizations. The passion for change and possibility dies, and a somnolent sleepwalking state of maintaining the status quo as a refuge against the chaos takes up residence in us.

The sleepwalking state is an expression of a leveling response humans use to reduce stress produced by ambiguity and tension. Seeking balance by leveling out differences and biases creates the relief of uniformity and reinforces community behavioral patters while minimizing stress. However, it also tends to inhibit innovation, change, chance, and creativity. For this reason, the artist has a bias toward the opposite response to tension, that of conceptual sharpening in which differences are not eliminated but seen as starting points for exploration and discovery. This process invites inquiry, experimentation, analogy, metaphor, and soul-filled imagination. Seen in context, leveling and sharpening are antithetical—one promotes convention, the other, invention. Art is the counterpoint to the pervasive leveling tendency of modern society in the face of change (Paratore, 1985).

In these chaotic times, the artist offers tremendous gifts to us, for all art is born out of chaos. Countering the tendency in American culture to banish, through medication or passive stimulation, all that gives us unease, pain, and suffering, the artist seeks out a meaningful relationship with it, knowing that some new form will be born out of the formlessness. The artist within each of us, as individuals and collectively in community, challenges us to restore our imaginative capacity "to adapt to change, to struggle," seeking creative resolution in the process.

Bruce Moon is such a seeker, an artist therapist who has lived and worked within the cultural milieu of psychological treatment for over twenty years. Decrying the somnolent state of convention, he proposes with urgency the need for "imaginative reclamation" that would return the artistic soul of psychology in order to connect psyche with artistic endeavors that bring meaning. However, as Moon writes:

> To think of this text as a call to reintroduce the arts to psychology is a mistake. It is not that artists should enter into psychotherapeutic work, for their work has always been inherently

psychotherapeutic. Rather, psychotherapists should enter into artistic work in order to rediscover the roots of their endeavors as art.

Moon acknowledges that this is a task that resists logical discussion, and indeed, in the climate of accountability that interprets all human behaviors through systems which restrict impulse, erase symptoms, quantify, analyze, pathologize, and objectively label, Moon is the quintessential rebel and heretic. To speak of art and soul as a reclamation project of vital importance to psychology is to call for cutting through our professional conditioning and bringing forth a courageous vision. And yet, his rebellious vision has an unexpectedly quiet and reflective presence. In this text, he paints the soul through art, imagery, and story, often digressing into deep pools or turbulent rivers of his experience that serve to build a steady vision dedicated to core values and beliefs. A reader seeking clear-cut and immediate truths may be too distracted by the wanderings of the soul-seeker. Giving space, or allowing the pattern of wholeness in Moon's words, stories, and reflections to well up and take shape, however, will yield a satisfying and inspiring experience.

Moon speaks of *taking care;* allowing the image to emerge and to take shape in its own time, and the vital need to give it sustained attention in order to come to know it deeply. Nor can one do this work without mastering the materials and processes of creative expression. The slower pace, rich texture, and resonant mood he speaks of from the studio of the artist therapist within a clinical setting seems to jar our senses, which may be more attuned to the realities of managed care, quick fixes, and revolving-door treatment. This contrast may create in the reader a profound ache of what Moon calls the "lost image of people as creative beings." A depth of longing stirred in waters of his reflections here resonates with the existential emptiness and loneliness of our times. In recognition of the blank canvas, poised in readiness to awaken to the struggle for some form being born, we face some aspect of our deaths in all the possibilities not chosen—the paintings not painted, the words not spoken, the lives not lived. This conflict, Moon reminds us, is a symbol of a life in process, infinitely preferred over keeping the struggle soulless and at bay.

Perhaps this text best can be described as an art therapist's journal of recurrent references and reflections born of authentic witness to the artistic struggle taught to him over time by clients engaged in the act of healing through art. Essentially a phenomenological work, Moon brings together critical ideas and human concerns that must not be lost. His trust in the process, sticking with his core beliefs, his willingness to return again and again to the essential phenomenon of the image in order to learn what it has to offer, and its recurrent verification in his life and the lives of his clients forms the basis of his artistic psychology. He sees these chapters not as empirical theory but rather as "imaginative reflections" and the client stories as "aesthetic fictions."

What emerges from the sensory, aesthetic, and existential phenomena and patterns of his life elaborates upon the cycle of life, death, and rebirth. He locates these as intersecting points where the soul lives, between the clinic and the home, the self and the other, the artist and the witness. The years of pain and struggle, whether his clients' or his own, does indeed seem to require an imaginative response, "the analogous level of human reply to the world." One finds him introducing most of the stories in these chapters at their very beginning, that is, the first encounter between the canvas and the individual's lonely and courageous act of making, as if to underscore the sacredness of that act. We learn that the artistic tradition of struggle, informed by the image from its very inception, brings honor to the unfoldings of imagination the act subsequently compels and gives form to. The beginning holds both death and rebirth, suspended in a single moment in time. Thus, the reader senses the poignancy and urgency of Moon "painting his way to safety" when he sees his own death and rebirth recurring in these essential materials of art, life, and soul.

Moon believes that images are living things, benevolent forces born of compassion, and that making art is powerful and good. This theme resonates through all his written work, a drumbeat found in *Existential Art Therapy: The Canvas Mirror, Essentials of Art Therapy Education and Practice, Introduction to Art Therapy: Faith in the Product, The Dynamics of Art as Therapy with Adolescents, Ethical Issues in Art Therapy,* and *Working with Images: The Art of Art Therapists. Art and Soul: Reflections on an Artistic Psychology* provides a meaningful frame for his core values and ideas, ultimately asking for a return to the deep human source that is imagination. Moon's earlier lament to the profession of art therapy, where is the art? has become a deeper cry, where is the soul? Not a material object, the artist's soul is rather a viewpoint that is an enlivened way of seeing the world ensouled in imagery. The compassion of art requires both courage and hope, to see the world as it is and to *imagine* it as it can become. For a world that can no longer imagine itself is a dead, lifeless place. Waking to life while embracing its death struggles, Moon believes the task at hand is to give form to the essential story of our particular life or time found in the images we create. His story helps us to find and create our story, and engenders in us reclaimed compassion, hope, and faith.

Lynn Kapitan, Ph.D., ATR-BC
Associate Professor
Chair of the Art Department
Mount Mary College
Milwaukee, Wisconsin

ACKNOWLEDGMENTS

I am deeply indebted to many people who have contributed to the writing of the second edition if this book. Thanks go to Cathy Moon for her work as the editor of the manuscript. Cathy's criticism and support were invaluable as I wrestled with the work. Special thanks also to my colleague, Dr. Lynn Kapitan, for reading the early manuscript and contributing the preface. When the first edition of this text was published, Lynn and I were distant colleagues. Now, at the publication of the second edition, we share a common office complex at Mount Mary College. Her good humor and sharp critiques have been precious. My buddy and pen pal, Dr. John Reece, with whom I shared a 10′ x 12′ office for many years, was a source of unconditional support. John's intelligent, creative, and witty emails and letters buoyed my spirits when the work was not going well. Ellie Jones, the editor of the first edition, has my deepest gratitude for her patience, skill, and interest in my writing.

I was honored for twenty-two years to be affiliated with Harding Hospital in Columbus, Ohio. The hospital merged with another hospital a couple years ago and I fear that much of the creativity, innovation, and dynamic modes of treatment pioneered there may be irretrievably lost. As the health care industry has undergone massive change and restructuring, I have felt particularly blessed by having had the opportunity to learn my craft at a unique period in the history of mental health care. Thanks to the many students I worked with in the

Harding Graduate Clinical Art Therapy program, Lesley College, Marywood University, and Mount Mary College. The students I've helped to educate and the colleagues I've argued and celebrated with have helped to shape my ideas about art and soul. Finally, I must express gratitude to the struggling artist-clients I've known. I have spent thousands of hours in the company of people who have been hurt, angry, and confused, and I have seen the power of art as a healing, calming, and sense-making force. These client-artists taught me most of what I know.

AUTHOR'S NOTE

The clinical accounts in this book are, in spirit, true. In all instances, however, identities and circumstances have been fictionalized in order to insure the confidentiality of the persons with whom I have worked. The case illustrations are amalgamations of many specific situations.

CONTENTS

ILLUSTRATIONS

ART AND SOUL

Figure 1. Let us imagine an artistic psychology, then, as a process of applying soulful artistic principles to everyday life.

INTRODUCTION

What I want to present in this book are ideas about soul restoration through art. Many of the emotional concerns I have heard from clients in the psychiatric hospital and in my private practice studio revolve around loss of soul. Loss of soul is experienced in emptiness, disillusionment, depression, longing for meaning, and a yearning for spirituality. Moore (1992) writes, "All these symptoms reflect a loss of soul and let us know what the soul craves" (p. xvi). Without soul, life is somehow vague and meaningless.

The artistic psychology presented in this book addresses the hungers people feel and the symptoms that torment them. By making art, it is possible to fill emptiness, rediscover wonder, ease depression, revive joy, create meaning, and practice a form of spiritual discipline.

This book is intended for artists and therapists who are willing to enter into the mysteries of lost souls. It is also intended for laypersons who may be suffering the symptoms of soul loss. It is my hope that therapists will rethink the work of the caregiver, and that sufferers will re-imagine the meaning of suffering. We have, for a long time, considered the work of therapy as secular, but if we really want to address the symptoms of soul loss, we now must begin to regard it as sacred art. Let us imagine an artistic psychology, then, as a process of applying soulful artistic principles to everyday life.

In the early years of my career as an art therapist I often heard professional colleagues express deep fears about the process of artistic expression. One psychiatrist was especially concerned because I encouraged his clients to draw what he described as "sick pictures." He thought that expressing troubling emotional material through creative visual, imaginal, form invited a lack of internal psychic control on the part of clients. On several occasions we discussed whether particular clients should be encouraged to express or to suppress their troubling feelings. I believe expression of feelings is seldom harmful to people, but keeping secrets and constricting feelings can be psychologically destructive.

My skeptical colleague expressed the belief that images (at least those produced by his clients) could be pathological. Pathological means "of or concerned with disease; governed by a compulsion" (Webster, 1988, p. 990). In contrast, I regard the artistic process of creating images as expression of *pathos,* that quality which evokes sympathy or compassion.

Whether artistic images are expressions of sickness and disease or expressions that evolve of sympathy and compassion is a pivotal philosophic question in an artistic psychology, for it represents the essential dilemma regarding the role of imagery and art making in therapy and in the world at large. There are, I believe, three basic modes of relating to and regarding imagery.

In the first mode, artwork is regarded as overt expressions of unconscious conflictive material. People who regard imagery in this way assert that particular psychological and pathological meanings can be ascribed to symbolic images. This way of relating to imagery has its roots in Freudian analysis. In this model, images are regarded as servants of the *id* and represent powerful sexual and aggressive drives. Those who subscribe to this way of considering imagery often attempt to classify and catalogue images. The effort to systematically classify images inevitably leads to equations regarding the meaning of particular images. From such a viewpoint, for instance, cylinders = phallic symbols; doorways = vaginal openings; lightning = rage; navels = dependency needs, and so on. Such formulas invariably focus on a disease orientation, or on dysfunctional aspects of the individual when viewing images. From this perspective, images are concrete representations of the sick or pathological.

A second mode of relating to imagery, which I refer to as diagnostic-psycho-stereotypical, stems from yet another pathological understanding of art products. In this approach to imagery, it is believed that persons with certain types of psychiatric disorders tend to create art in which the content and/or style is indicative of diagnostic classification. When a therapist who ascribes to this approach sees the art works of a given individual, the therapist may hypothesize about the appropriate diagnosis for the individual. For instance, if a therapist operating from the diagnostic-psycho-stereotypical school of thought believes that clients suffering from depression typically use only a small portion of the picture plane when given a choice, it follows that when the therapist observes a client restricting use of the page, she might hypothesize the client is depressed.

A person is seldom diagnosed as healthy and functional. The process of psychological diagnosis is reserved for those whom we view as ill. In other words, to approach imagery from a diagnostic-psycho-stereotypifying perspective implies a belief that images are manifestations of disease.

At the other philosophic pole from these pathologizing positions are the views of Allen (1995), McConeghey (1986), McNiff (1992), Moon (1995), and others. In his lectures and workshops, McNiff offers the maxim, "the image never comes to hurt you." From his perspective, images are viewed as benevolent forces born of compassion. Artistic psychology is based upon the principle that images are benevolent and compassionate entities.

In my work with graduate art therapy students at colleges

and universities throughout the country, I have often encountered the benevolent power of images. One student was particularly disturbed by recurring images of walls that emerged in her drawings. The walls appeared in artwork she made in therapy sessions with clients and in classroom group experiences. Initially, she thought the walls represented her style of compartmentalizing various aspects of her life. This walling-off seemed to serve a defensive and constricting function in her life. I encouraged her to think of the walls as friendly messengers rather than to interpret them as symbols of repressed, conflictive psychic material or indicators of pathological dysfunction. As the student engaged in imaginative dialogue with the walls, she began to think of them as an invitation to loosen her tight and compartmentalized emotional control. Over the course of her graduate training, the sharp edges and harsh dividing walls in her artworks softened and gave way to images of fluidity and flexibility.

Artistic psychology embraces the belief that images have lives of their own. Images are creations, of course, and in a sense are reflections of their creator, but they are more. As a demonstration of this, I suggest the following experiment. Invite an artist and ten other people to create, independent of one another, a story about one of the artist's works. I assure you ten different stories will emerge, and each will be different from the story the artist would tell. The artwork speaks to each person differently.

Images may be thought of as messengers or intermediaries. McNiff (1992) describes images as "artistic angels" (pp. 74–88). When we regard images as messengers, they cease to be objects of inquiry and become subjects capable of teaching us about ourselves.

When we regard images as messengers, having lives of their own, then we may consider them as having missions of their own as well. Artistic psychology considers restoration of soul to be one of the missions of images. When working from the perspective of an artistic psychology, based upon the notion of images as benevolent and compassionate entities, we are dealing with living images and the living artists who make them. Both subjects, the artist and the image, command deep respect.

In an artistic psychology, it is impossible to establish formulas for interpretation of images or equations for analysis. To do so would be akin to performing an autopsy on the image, and we know autopsies are only performed on the dead. In artistic psychology, *this* does not always mean *that*. Artworks and images are not cadavers to be measured, dissected, and biopsied. The world of artistic imagination is, at times, one of mist and shadows. Those who would attend to this world must embrace the mystery and cultivate a sense of reverential seeing. Our work often takes us into ambiguous places where nothing is absolute.

We have the option of thinking of images as infectious and diseased, or of regarding them as living, ensouled entities worthy of tender care and respect. The choice we make colors every aspect of our work with images. I urge compassion over dissection, pathos over pathology.

There are many lost souls in the world, people who feel empty though they have much in terms of material possessions. They are disillusioned, though their world appears complete. They feel vaguely sad all the time. They long for some enduring sense of purpose and they yearn for some deeper connection to the world. Perhaps art offers an antidote. Perhaps people who are lost souls can fill their own emptiness, rediscover their sense of wonder, recover joy, and create meaning through the discipline of making art.

In artistic psychology, it is important to embrace an aesthetic of everyday matters. In letting go of familiarity and a position of knowing, imagination has the opportunity to enter in, allowing questions to arise in concerning the interrelationships of art, image, and soul. Among these questions are: What is art? What is image? What is soul?

Like so many other questions that confound and confuse, attempts to address them inevitably unearth many other questions buried beneath the surface: What purposes do images and souls serve? Is imagination necessary? Can imagination and soul be rationally studied? What is life like without imagination, without art, without soul? What do they have to do with one another?

All persons must choose. Will we choose to live life in the shallow regions? Or will we take hold of the opportunities before us to increase our sensitivity, heighten our awareness, and live responsibly in the face of overwhelming change? Will we seek restoration of soul through art?

These questions intrigue, challenge, and baffle me. Still, I believe they are worth asking and so I will follow them where they lead. It is important for readers of this book to note that when I refer to art and art making, I do so from a modernist perspective. I am aware that ideas about what art is are being challenged and expanded by postmodernist aestheticians. While postmodern perspectives are of interest to me, I am not prepared to integrate them in this text.

Many of the illustrative case vignettes in this book involve painting and drawing tasks. These vignettes reflect my personal experience with drawing and painting, but in no way should this be construed as a diminishing of other equally valid artistic endeavors. I simply have to write about those experiences with which I am most familiar and competent.

Figure 2. To whom does one turn for support in matters of the soul?

Chapter I

SOUL LOSS–LOST SOUL

At the beginning of the twenty-first century, we are living in a time of great transformation. Old ways of thinking about the world and our place in it are fading away; new ways are not yet clear. Evidence of change is all around us. The basic structures of society—family, gender roles, educational systems, religion, and cultural identity—have undergone tremendous change. Communications technology, economic globalization, the labor market, and countless other aspects of life have undergone radical shifts in a very short time. The tragic events of September 11, 2001, have shaken the sense of stability formerly enjoyed by American citizens, which has had a ripple effect in other countries.

There are choices to be made. Should we withdraw into ourselves out of anxiety and fear? Scared by the loss of our familiar ways of being in the world, will we become immobilized, thinking only of ourselves? Will we choose to live life in the shallow regions? Or will we take hold of the opportunities before us to increase our sensitivity, heighten our awareness, and live responsibly in the face of overwhelming change? Will we seek restoration of soul?

This book is a call for restoration of soul. To live soulfully means to embrace the unknown, to welcome mystery. This way of living requires creativity and courage.

Perhaps the most common disorder of the second half of

the twentieth century and the beginning of the twenty-first, affecting society, families, and individuals, is existential emptiness. In 1953, Viktor Frankl described this phenomenon as the "existential vacuum" (p. 128). More recently, Hillman (1989), Moore (1992), McNiff (1992), and others have referred to this as loss of soul. Loss of soul, or existential emptiness, is acted out in the world through dysfunctional relationships, boredom, abuse of self and others, addictions, and a pervasive sense that life has no purpose. People suffering from loss of soul feel unexplainable emptiness. They are disillusioned in their relationships and in their work. They feel vaguely depressed and they long for meaning in their lives. Often, they yearn for some kind of spirituality in their lives. Therapists, politicians, social scientists, and television talk-show hosts suggest a variety of theories regarding the causes and antidotes for these symptoms. But the root problem is soul loss.

To whom does one turn for support in matters of the soul? Where does one go to fill the existential vacuum? Many people in the psychology professions have distanced themselves from aspects of humanness not subject to the scientific method. Health care institutions have adopted the mindset and values of capitalist corporations; have become profit-driven instead of service-focused. Soul restoration and emptiness filling are not profitable.

To whom does one turn for support in matters of the soul? In our collective past, there is a remarkable wellspring of insights from people who have lived their lives in contact with soul: painters, poets, musicians, sculptors, dancers, and playwrights. In this book, I will explore how making art can fill existential emptiness, and how imagining and creating restores soul.

When I refer to soul in this context, I am describing a perspective, a way of looking at things and events, and a way of being in the world. I am not referring to soul as a thing or substance somehow connected to life beyond this world. Soul is found wherever imaginative work is underway. Soul has to do with meaning, authenticity, and the deep regions of shadow and light. Soul is most visible in creative work, love, intimacy, and community.

In the twenty-nine years I have practiced art therapy, I have been intrigued by how useful my studies in literature, poetry, and the arts have been. So it is that I suggest we must turn to image, story, movement, rhyme, and metaphor for guidance in this troubled, empty, and soul-less time if we are to have hope of easing the suffering of empty, bored, and frightened souls.

Freud suggested psychoanalysis was better understood and applied by writers and artists than by doctors (Papini, 1934). A central theme of this book is a call to–at least temporarily–disengage thoughts of the psyche/soul from the realm of empirical science and bring them back to the heart of the artist.

James Hillman, a prominent voice of Archetypal Psychology, introduced the idea that soul is a perspective that changes random events into meaningful experiences (1989). Transforming casual encounters into significant experiences is what artists have done throughout time. The artist catches a glimpse of the face of a passerby. In the moment, the glimpse means nothing. Later, in her studio, she devotes hours of intensive labor to crafting a painting of the stranger she passed on the street. By investing her time, attention, and talent, she imbues the insignificant passing-by with meaning. Through her artistic endeavor, she ensouls the random happening.

Perhaps what is most needed in our present day is the capacity to stop, consider, and reflect upon the common everyday events of our lives. The therapy most needed at this time consists of reacquainting people with their capacities to imagine and create meaning. In order to do this, we must communicate in the language of the imagination: pictures, songs, dances, and dreams. Imagination is the fundamental expressive tool of soul.

Soul is found in midpoints of experience; between understanding and intuition, fact and fiction, desire and action. As the artist stands before the canvas, she stands in the midpoint, between imagination and reality. The alchemical interplay between the two is given form on the canvas.

> . . . *between the moonlight and the lane*
> *the sailboat and the drain*
> *the newsreel and your tiny pain*
> *love calls you by your name*
> Leonard Cohen (1968)

Authentic relationships, satisfying work, and personal meaning are manifestations of *ensoulment*. Relief from boredom, anxiety, depression, and addictions are the pleasant side effects of engaging the imagination, and of restoring the soul. Unfortunately, meaningful work and satisfying relationships are elusive phenomena at this time, for imagination and soul have been ascribed little value in our culture. Imagination has been relegated to the realm of pretending and left to children. Indeed, adults who too obviously indulge their imaginations are sometimes chided for being "childish." Soul has been abandoned as unverifiable, immeasureable, and unprofitable. All too often we know of soul mainly by its absence; in the void, in the boredom, and in the pain we feel even when we have everything we could want.

Surely there must be a way to fill the emptiness, kindle interest, ease the pain, and restore the soul. It is evident that cognitive and behavioral therapy approaches cannot get us through these discontents, because behaviors and thoughts are part of the difficulty. We long to ensoul our lives and we yearn to rediscover our imaginations and our capacities to make.

This book is about imagination reclamation, soul restoration. It is about making soul and reinvigorating life. There is nothing new in these ideas. Philosophers, theologians, poets, musicians, painters, dancers, and archetypal psychologists have offered glimpses of a soulful, cavernous region inhabited by passionate, mysterious images. I am simply revisiting a very old idea, that soul is important in our lives. I am proposing art making as a means to return soul to life.

It is imperative that imagination be restored to the foreground of our lives. It is time for imagination and soul to take center-stage. It is our responsibility, yours and mine, to care for imagination and to attend to our collective soul.

The Greek root word for therapy is best translated, "to be attentive to." If we are to be truly responsible for ourselves, then each individual must attend to his or her own psyche (soul); must be his/her own therapist. However, due to the circumstances of one's life, this may not always be possible. When one is incapable of attending to soul in a caring and nurturing manner, a therapeutic relationship is needed in order to restore the capacity to care for self.

To begin, we must restructure our thinking about the indicators of existential emptiness. Rather than regard disillusionment, meaninglessness, angst, boredom, or depression as emotional tumors requiring surgical removal, we can view these manifestations of emptiness as gifts from the soul, meant to shake us into life. In this way, emotional turmoil may be seen as a "precious angel" bringing a critical message (Hillman, 1989). Certainly we would not wish to have an *angelectomy;* to have the angel cut out. When we think of emotional turmoil as a gift, we do not need to cure it, fix it, or banish it. On the contrary, we are obliged to listen to the messages our imagination has for us.

In order to listen for the messages our intermediaries bring us, we need to exercise our imagination. If we hope to find meaning in the everyday events of our lives, we must cultivate new ways of reflecting upon these events. We must use our imagination and our capacities to create.

The Greek word *psyche* means soul; *ology* refers to "the study of." Therefore *psychology* means study of the soul. This book is an effort to return psychological thought to these roots, to reclaim the artistic and imaginative ground of psychological thinking.

In western culture, art, spirituality, psychology, therapy, and religion have been divided and defended against one another for a long time. There is evidence that renewed interest is stirring toward bridging the gaps between these sister elements. Psychology, spirituality, psychotherapy, and organized religion are all in need of new visions if they are to hope for continued relevance and potency in this postmodern world.

Reflections on an artistic psychology call us toward a different regard for imagination and art making in our lives. This new regard is modeled after the artist's attention, intuition, and sensitivity. Being called is not easy, and there is no set path to follow. Imagination does not come back into one's life just because it is invited. It must be crafted, worked with, played with, and struggled with.

In this book, I am not proposing a cure for emotional turmoil and I am not advocating the elimination of scientific psychology. On the contrary, I want to suggest ways to embrace emotional turmoil that may be beyond the scope of cognitive behaviorism and psychopharmacology. The artistic psychology I am proposing is not meant to aid in anyone's adjustment to cultural or familial norms, but rather to facilitate attachment to the deep root of inner life, the imagination.

In the mid-seventies, a client told me, "My pictures are the windows to my soul." At the time, I thought she was merely being poetic. Now, three decades later, I understand the profound meaning of her words. She knew then what it has taken me so long to learn. It makes sense to me now that she routinely chose to stay in the art studio rather than attend verbal group therapy sessions. Her difficulties were the direct result of a withered imagination. It was in the studio that she restored her soul.

If you have come to this book in search of a road map, you

will be frustrated. Imagination and soul defy topography. If you have come seeking interstate highways, prepare yourself for gravel roads and overgrown paths. I offer no rules to live by.

If a dream would never end and a road would never bend
I wouldn't have this feeling now
But the morning sun will burn and a highway must turn
I wouldn't want to change it anyhow

Moon, 1976

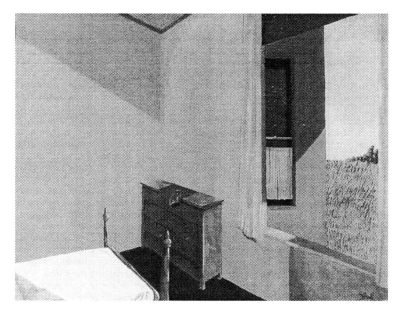

Figure 3. Emptiness, boredom, depression, and a longing for meaning . . .

Chapter II

SYMPTOMS OF SOUL LOSS

L et us now turn to the indications of soul loss: emptiness, boredom and depression, and a longing for meaning.

Emptiness

The process of using one's imagination and art making as a method of soul restoration inevitably leads to the awareness that each person is ultimately alone. Although I often paint in the company of my clients, students, and colleagues, making art is ultimately a lonely enterprise. I look at the empty surface of the canvas and I am reminded of how alone I really am. The stretched canvas calls me to free it from its emptiness. As I brush color across the surface, something deep within me resonates.

The symptom of emptiness often emerges in psychotherapy sessions in the guise of loneliness. Loneliness is such a common complaint that it seems almost unnecessary to discuss it. Still, I want to reflect upon it from an artistic psychological perspective in order to demonstrate how art making responds to, and transforms, emptiness and loneliness.

I encounter two kinds of emptiness in my clinical work. First, emptiness is embodied in loneliness between persons. Interpersonal emptiness is marked by the sense of being isolated from others. This kind of loneliness can be brought on by a variety of external conditions such as conflict in relationships, inadequate social abilities, or physical separation from significant others. Interpersonal emptiness is seen time and again in art therapy studios.

The second form of emptiness has to do with separation from one's own imaginal inner life. For our purposes here, I will refer to this as *intrinsic loneliness.* Intrinsic loneliness is a sense of separation inherent within persons.

People often feel estranged from others, but beneath this separation is a fundamental loneliness that is deeper than interpersonal emptiness. Intrinsic aloneness, or separation from soul, often exists regardless of the presence of relationships with significant others. Intrinsic loneliness is experienced as a chasm between the self and meaningful experiences in life. This form of emptiness was poignantly portrayed by Dustin Hoffman's character, Ben, in the movie *The Graduate.* In one scene, Ben is wearing a scuba diving suit he had received as a birthday gift. He is being forced to perform for his parents and their friends at his birthday party. The camera offers a view from behind the scuba mask, while Ben peers out at his parents and their friends. No sound is heard except the mechanical breathing apparatus. Ben is surrounded, yet utterly alone as he sinks to the bottom of the pool. In my work, I have often encountered clients who have sealed off aspects of themselves and become detached from their own essential creative nature, their soul.

THE STORY OF KATE

Kate had a Master's of Fine Arts degree, but she told me she didn't make art anymore. There was deep sadness in her eyes that I sensed was not new for her. She spoke quietly, almost as if she was apologizing for speaking at all. She was not sure she really wanted to be in therapy.

I suggested we work together to build a canvas. She said, "But I told you, I don't make art anymore."

"Kate, you called me. You came, and I believe it will be helpful if we work on something together rather than just sit and talk. If you decide you don't want to come back, at least you will have a new canvas."

As we worked during that first session, her eyes held a haunted look. She said, "I'm still not exactly sure why I am here, Dr. Moon."

"I don't know *exactly* why you've come to me either, Kate, and by the way, you can call me Bruce. My hunch is, it has something to do with things you can't talk about right now. Could you hold these two by two's while I nail them together?" She put a hand on each piece of wood, well away from the corner. "Kate," I said, "you'll never be able to hold them tight enough that way. You have to hold them closer to the corner. Trust me, I won't hit you with the hammer."

She grimaced. "I know how to build a canvas!" But she adjusted her hands.

"Ok, that's good," I said, and began to nail the corners together. "I will not hit you with the hammer. You don't make art anymore?"

"I haven't had time," she replied.

"So you have the time now, Kate?"

"Yes, too much time." As these words were spoken, her eyes brimmed with tears. We worked in silence.

For the rest of the session, we stretched and stapled canvas, and then she covered the canvas with gesso.

"Time's up, Kate. If you want to come again, next week, same time is ok with me."

"I guess I'd like to come back, but I don't think I will be able to paint anything."

"I know that feeling, Kate. Whatever you do will be fine. You are welcome here," I said.

When Kate entered the studio the following week, I was

working on a large painting. The work was not going well and I was not happy about it. She looked around the studio. "Are all these paintings yours?"

"Some of them are. Some are by students, some by clients."

"They're nice," she said.

"Thanks, Kate. So, where do you need to begin?"

"I just want to mess around with those things." She pointed toward a shelf filled with sticks, feathers, glitter, stones, empty prescription bottles, twine, wire, tissue paper . . . stuff.

"Mess away," I said. "But if you'd like to use the canvas we built last week, it is over there." I pointed at the canvas.

"Are you telling me I should use the canvas?" She asked.

"No. Whatever you do will be welcome here," I said. A tear slid down her cheek. "Your tears are welcome here."

She stood and began to gather objects from the shelf.

* * * * *

In the next session, Kate gathered stones, some sticks, a feather, and a small piece of shiny blue foil. At first she simply held these things, but then she began to place them in relationship to one another. She asked, "Is that the same painting you were working on last week?"

I sighed. "Yes, it is."

"It certainly changed. What is it going to be?"

"I am not sure," I replied. I am thinking about painting the whole canvas black and then starting over.

She looked up from where she was sitting with her collection of objects, "What will go on the black?" She asked.

As I thought about her question, it occurred to me that nothing would go on the black. I said, "I think something has to come out of the black."

"Out of the void!" She laughed. As her words left her lips, images began to appear in my mind's eye.

Kate stood and took a step away from the table where she had been working. I looked at what she had done. A circle of stones surrounded the blue shimmering foil. A feather lay gently on one side of the circle. A big stick stood awkwardly on the other side. She looked at her work and said, "That's it."

I responded, "Tell me the story."

She shook her head. "It is not time yet."

I looked. I waited. I said, "Reminds me of an oasis."

Kate said, "This is my void. Aren't we about out of time?"

"Just about," I said. Kate's face was flushed. She was sweating. I asked, "Do you want to say anything else about your construction?"

"No."

"Well, do you want to put it on a board, so we can keep it till next session?"

"No. I will just put the pieces back where they belong."

I said, "Your pieces are welcome here."

* * * * *

For several months Kate came to the studio every week. She arranged stones, sticks, bits of fabric, and small bits of hardware. She often backed away from the table so we could look at these things together. She did not have much to say. At the end of one session, Kate said, "I think I will just leave this the way it is."

I responded, "You aren't going to take it apart?"

"No, I will just leave it here."

I said, "It is welcome here."

Kate said, "I believe you."

* * * * *

Kate entered the studio. She said, "I've been thinking a lot about my art, and about the work I've done here."

"Me too," I replied.

"I am thinking maybe I won't need to come here too much longer." Her eyes sparkled. "Would you like me to paint today?"

"You are free to do whatever you'd like to do," I said.

"I will miss you," she said. And then she gathered sticks and stones and buttons and thread and a piece of cotton fabric. She arranged the sticks and stones and buttons on the cloth. And then, she sewed. I painted.

As time was running out, I said to her, "Kate, we really ought to talk about what you said about leaving therapy."

"Yes, we should. I've been thinking I'd like to come about three more times. That will be enough for me."

"Why three?" I asked.

She smiled. "Three's my lucky number."

She told me a story about her sticks and stones, buttons and cloth. I listened. Each stick was a member of her family tree. Each stone an incident. Each button a disappointment. These were the things sewn tightly to the cloth of her life.

Near the end of the session I asked, "Are you going to leave this piece behind?"

She paused. "No, I think I will take it with me."

* * * * *

Kate entered the studio. She was carrying a large roll of canvas. She was jumpy, bubbly, filled with energy. "I have a surprise," she said. She unrolled the canvas. It must have been ten feet long, five feet wide. Colors screamed, shapes exploded, and overlapping lines bound it all together. The image of an angel dancing, or flying, beckoned. Painted renderings of her sticks, stones, were joined with planets and birds, and shooting stars surrounding the angel. I was speechless. All I could say was, "Yowsa!" Kate giggled.

"Do you like it?"

"Like it? Kate, this is . . . this is . . . amazing."

She laughed. "I've been working on it for awhile. I wanted it to be done before we finished up."

I rubbed my eyes, astonished. "I thought you couldn't paint anymore."

"I never said I couldn't. I said I didn't."

We sat together for several minutes just looking at her painting, and then at mine. On my canvas there was a new image, a snake of fire winding into the distance. I thought of how in Kansas they burn the old prairie grass so that new grass can grow, so the cattle will be fed. Fire, cleansing . . . the inside . . . my heart.

* * * * *

Last session. Kate wanted to work on the canvas we'd made in her first session. She wanted us both to paint, and so we did. The image that came was of a coyote on an island, surrounded by rendered sticks, stones, bits of cloth, and hardware. She said, "You know, when you go to the funeral of somebody who really lived life fully and completely, there is little sadness–much joy. This day is sort of like that kind of funeral, Bruce. We were here, we didn't hold back. We gave, we received, we lived fully . . . everything was completely welcome here."

* * * * *

I am not sure exactly what Kate's artistic works meant. But I am sure she rekindled her enthusiasm for life by arranging sticks and stones, buttons and string . . . ordinary things. She ensouled these simple objects. Through her constructions and paintings, she created a relationship with me and restored her soul. She became reacquainted with her capacity to make and to have meaning, and in so doing she eased the empty loneliness she had felt for a long time.

Boredom and Depression

Being devoid of interest, *utterly bored,* is one of the most prevalent and malevolent of the afflictions faced by many modern people, but it is a relatively new phenomenon in the history of humankind. For much of our collective past, we have been too busy to be bored. Prior to the industrial revolution, people had to be creative in order to survive. They made their own clothes, shelter, food, and entertainment. It is an appropriate footnote to the concept of the survival of the fittest that being "fit" denotes being creative.

Since the western industrial revolution, we have been given tremendous amounts of leisure time. However, many people have no idea about how to fill their unstructured hours.

One can easily see how television has become so popular a medium. It requires little effort, little thought, and asks for no response. Hours can figuratively be killed through passive non-involvement. The imagination, like muscle, atrophies if neglected.

SARA'S SOLE

Sara shuffled through the door to the creative arts studio at the psychiatric hospital. She sat with her head down on the table. What I knew about Sara from her intake report was that she was diagnosed with depression. She had come to the hospital directly from an emergency room where her stomach had been pumped. She had overdosed on alcohol and over-the-counter sleeping pills. She was seventeen. The intake report quoted her parents. "She is out of control . . . we don't even know her anymore." The report also quoted Sara as saying, "Life sucks."

"Sara," I said, "my name is Bruce. Welcome to the art studio." She did not move.

"Here in the studio, Sara, we use art as a way of expressing feelings. Let me show you around the building." I stepped away as if to begin the tour of the creative arts building. Sara turned her head so that she could see me.

"You don't need to bother showing me around. I ain't gonna do anything anyway. Jus' let me be."

"Well, Sara, I know it must be a little hard being here your first day. I've got some things I need to do. I'll stop back in a little while. Okay?"

She yawned. "This is so boring."

"Sara, do you know where boredom comes from?"

"Huh?"

"Boredom comes from an absence of quality relationships." She did not comment.

When I returned to the table where she was slumped, I asked, "Sara, are you ready for the tour now?" She said nothing but feigned a snore.

The next two sessions went like the first. Sara was passive, bored, and disengaged. It was as if she had turned on the "No Vacancy" sign, locked the doors, and pulled the shades on her life.

At that time, I was working on a painting of the basement of the house where I grew up. My mother had died about six months earlier and the image recalled powerful memories. When I was very small, my mom did laundry for other people in order to support the family. The old-fashioned wringer washer was in the basement and I spent countless hours there with her in my pre-school years. She worked and I played basketball.

The first time Sara showed any interest in what was going on around her, she looked up from her table and asked, "Why's that bushel basket hangin' on the door?" I hesitated, moved away from my canvas, and replied, "When I was three or four years old, Sara, my mother gave me a basketball for my birthday. She put the basket on the door so I could have something to shoot at. I spent a lotta hours in this basement dribbling and shooting when I was little."

"You sound sad," Sara said.

"Well, my mother had a stroke last summer and died. I still miss her. This is a hard painting to make."

She frowned. "Then why are you painting it, if it makes you sad?"

"Hmmm. I guess I have to, Sara."

"Huh?"

"I have to. Sometimes images just come into my head and they won't go away until I do something with them."

"But it makes you sad?"

"Yes." I replied. "But I think that's what art is all about. It's taking the things that are important, or even just little things, and working with them. Sometimes they are sad things, or angry, or hurtful. It doesn't matter what the feeling is; painting helps me handle things in my life."

She sat back in her chair, "That's cool!" The next day Sara entered the studio and stood beside my easel. "Bruce, I want you to teach me how to paint." She pushed her hair away from her eyes. "I have a picture in my head that bothers me a lot. I want to see if you are right about handling things."

"Good, Sara. What size do you want your painting to be?"

"I get to choose?"

"Sure. We have to build the canvas so you can make it however you want, within reason, of course."

She grimaced. "But I thought I'd be able to start painting today. Can't we just use a canvas that's already made?"

"Some people buy canvas already stretched, Sara, but I think that's would be a mistake for you."

"But it would be a lot faster!"

I put down my brush. "Yes, I suppose it would be a lot faster. Sometimes, though, the point is not do things as quickly as possible. I think it would be better for you to take your time and really be a part of the whole process. In some ways, I wish I could teach you how to make your own paints."

"God, you sound like my Grandpa. He always says it's better to walk than to run, and better to drive than take the train, and better to take the train than fly."

"You're right, Sara. I do sound like that sometimes. Now what size do you want your canvas to be?"

She thought for a moment, "I want it to be a rectangle, hmm, let's say about three feet long and two feet high."

"Sounds good to me."

I taught Sara how to use the miter saw to cut 2 x 2s at 45 degree angles. It took her an hour to do it, but I was encouraged. Watching the sweat roll down her cheeks was a refreshing change from seeing her head down on the table in a pretense at sleep. The following day, I helped her nail the pieces of her stretcher frame together.

"Now do we put the canvas on?" She asked.

"No," I said. "Now you have to make braces for your frame. You probably need two or three of them."

"Not more sawing," she moaned.

"More sawing." I smiled.

On the next day, she began to stretch canvas over the frame she had built. I arrived at the studio a few minutes late and by the time I saw what she was doing she was nearly half done. However, she wasn't pulling the canvas tight enough. The canvas was rippled.

"Sara, you look like you are hurrying a bit."

"I want to paint today so I am working as quickly as I can."

"We have a problem. Do you see these ripples here? That means that you haven't pulled the canvas tight enough. I'm afraid you have to pull out your staples and start over."

She stared at me with an expression half rage, half incredulity. "You gotta be shittin' me."

"No, I'm talking straight. C'mon, I'll help." I started to pull staples. Reluctantly Sara helped me remove all of the staples. "Now, here's how to get it tight enough."

When we finished stretching, I showed her how to gesso the surface. "Tomorrow, you can start to paint."

When she arrived at the studio she was carrying a battered and worn black tennis shoe.

"What's with the shoe?" I asked her.

"This is what I want to paint. Well, sort of anyway. I've been having a dream with a shoe like this in it."

"What else will be going on in the picture?"

"Not much," se sighed. "It's really just this shoe lying on its side on a table. In the dream there is a spider crawling out of a hole in the sole. Where do I start?"

"What do you see in the background?"

"It's like a dirty brown wall."

"Okay, try to mix up some dirty brown. I'd suggest using burnt umber, yellow ochre and a touch of black. Just play around, see if you can get the color you want."

The image that emerged over several sessions was a hauntingly stark portrait of a decrepit basketball shoe. From a dark cavity in the tattered sole a menacing black spider crawled. As the days passed, Sara initiated conversation more often. Usually she would begin asking some technical question about painting, but she gradually shared more about her life and became increasingly interested in mine.

On one afternoon, as she neared completion of her shoe-sole painting, she said, "I'm sorry about your mom."

I stepped away from my canvas. "I wasn't sure you were really listening when I told you the story of this painting."

"I was." She looked at the floor. "I ain't never had anyone I love die, but I figure it must be like when I got cut from the basketball team, only a lot worse."

I gazed at her spider. "Yes, it's probably a little like that I guess. It must have been hard for you to be cut."

I could see the tears well in her eyes.

"It was like gettin' kicked in the stomach. Over and over again."

"Is that when the troubles started for you, Sara?"

"Not really, but it was like the last straw. I just quit caring about anything." Nothing more was said in that session.

In a profound way, the image of the basketball sole might

be thought of as an image of Sara's soul. The sole of the shoe was wounded. From the wound emerged a frightening image. Rather than keep walking with her woundedness, Sara had shut down. She quit trying. As she said, the image of a spider and a worn basketball shoe was, "a picture in my head that bothers me a lot." The picture, disturbing as it was, was also a messenger bearing the message that life goes on, in spite of the rejections and wounds we all endure. Sara's ability to imagine the scene, in the context of our relationship, re-established her liveliness. She ennobled the basketball shoe sole, and restored soul.

This imaginal work could not have been done in verbal psychotherapy. Sara's boredom and resistance would have thwarted efforts to engage in therapeutic conversation. It was essential for Sara to encounter, and revive herself through the experience of making art. This is not to diminish the therapeutic benefit of the relationship we developed, but our relationship was intimately connected to the creative process and engagement with art materials.

Regardless of when or why imagination is neglected, it is in fact left untended in some people. Following adolescence come the demands of early adulthood: establishing a solid identity, selecting a profession, finding a significant other, and perhaps bearing and raising children. Except for the very few, making and creating for the sake of expression and pleasure fades into memory.

Boredom and depression seep into leisure hours like a malignant fog. At first unclear and indefinite, they gradually form a thick, slippery, deadening veil. The only beam powerful enough to pierce the fog comes from within the individual in the form of imagination. Art making is an exciting process of shining through the fog, *ensouling* life and restoring imagination.

Conflict and Depression

Plato described music as the medicine of the soul that could raise the spirits of persons suffering from hopelessness. Renaissance writers referred to *melancholia* as a mental affliction characterized by extreme depression. The *Diagnostic and Statistical Manual of Mental Disorders IV* describes dysthymic disorder as, "Depressed mood (or can be irritable mood in children and adolescents) for most of the day, more days than not . . ." (1994, p. 169). No matter how they are described, or what they are called, despair and loss of hope are profoundly painful and disturbing. They bring intense inner conflict.

Conflict is everywhere in the world of the artist. The artistic response to conflict is to seek it, rather than attempt to avoid it, for art often comes not out of harmony and peace, but out of dissonance and emotional turmoil.

Life begins in struggle. The pre-birth hours are filled with dramatic movement away from the safety and warmth of the womb, toward the bright, cold uncertainty of life outside. The birth process is the first fearful and conflictive experience in the life of a person and it symbolizes much of what is to follow, a life composed of one conflict after another.

JEFF'S DESPAIR

Some time ago, a young man was referred to an expressive art therapy group I was leading in the community. The referring physician's consultation note said the client had been in individual psychotherapy for many months and had been in a short-term hospital treatment unit for adolescents for several weeks, but had made little progress because of his rigid defense system. In talking about the situation further with the psychiatrist, I learned that the client often skipped his psychotherapy sessions. When he did attend, he would often abruptly walk out after a few minutes. The psychiatrist was frustrated by this fourteen-year-old's antagonistic attitude, which was best summed up in the client's words, "Leave me the hell alone!"

The therapist had tried several treatment approaches in attempts to "hook" Jeff. At first, he had assumed a non-directive, passive demeanor. When no headway was made, he tried to be actively supportive and friendly. This provided Jeff with many opportunities to reject the therapist and devalue the process. Then the therapist shifted to a more controlling and confrontive mode, but this served only to increase Jeff's resistance to self-exploration and sharing. Jeff was mired in a hostile and resistive stance. His family's financial resources were being drained and the psychiatrist was afraid that time was running out for Jeff.

Jeff's history of problems included vandalism, truancy, violence, drug and alcohol abuse, and incorrigibility at home. The psychiatrist believed that beneath these behaviors, Jeff was quite depressed. The family feared that Jeff would end up in jail, or dead, if he did not make significant changes in his life. As I thought about Jeff's entry into the group, I made note of the many failed therapeutic interventions. I decided I would avoid confrontation whenever possible and try to engage Jeff exclusively through the metaphors of his images, whatever they might be. I hoped to be able to provide him with avenues for expressing the deep feelings that underlay his antisocial and self-defeating behaviors.

In the first session Jeff attended, I began by asking the group members to cover their large (3' x 3') papers with two colors that would somehow express the mood they had been in over the last few days. They were then asked to blend these colors together, making a solid background surface. Jeff was dubious and made several quiet, hostile, and devaluing comments to his peers. However, since everyone else in the group was working at the task, Jeff went along. I overheard his hostile comments but did not intervene or respond to his negativity. It seemed to me that the unspoken message of his peers' involvement was a stronger statement to him than anything I could say.

When the members of the group had completely covered their papers with color, I said, "Now we have a background for your drawings. Your task is to create whatever sort of image that comes to mind that would also express your feelings." Jeff seemed to like this idea. He picked up a black chalk and wrote in bold letters, "Leave Me Alone!" He then added drawings of the anarchy symbol, a smoldering fire, a whiskey bottle, and what appeared to be a pool of blood. He sneered to the boy sitting next to him, "That is the blood of the last asshole that fucked with me."

As others in the group talked about their drawings, I made every attempt to honor their images. When it was Jeff's turn to talk about his drawing, I commented (staying with the metaphor) that it looked like he had some very hard experiences.

Jeff said, "Wha' do ya' mean?"

I responded, "Well, if that is blood near the bottom of the page, it looks like someone has been hurt. And, and I see that you have had some experience with alcohol."

"Ah, screw this, man. This is a joke." Jeff quickly looked to his peers for support of his resistive attitude.

"Jeff," I said, "in this group I always take things that are drawn very seriously."

Jeff sneered, "Nice try. Go be therapeutic with some other sucker. I just drew this piece of crap. It don't mean a thing."

"It's fine with me if that's what you think, Jeff. But I believe that what we draw is kind of a self-portrait. A portrait of you." Jeff glared at me. I went on, "Of course, I don't know what to make of this 'Leave me alone' stuff. You do realize that I cannot do that, right? I mean, it's a professional impossibility."

"What the fuck are you talking about?"

"Jeff, you do realize it is not possible for me to leave you alone. I mean, I think you need me." At this, Jeff and the other boys in the group began to laugh uncomfortably. I laughed too. Then I shifted attention back to the image. "But really, Jeff, I see blood in your drawing and it makes me think really hurtful things must have happened in this picture."

"Yeah, so what?"

"It looks like this is a hard place, Jeff. But there is the fire that makes me think of warm things too. I'm glad you have it. It seems like you have needed your fire to protect you."

Jeff said, "Yeah, I s'pose."

This was the beginning of Jeff's journey into himself. Over the next few months, he led me down a path past horrible scenes of conflict with his father. Episodes of destructive acting out were represented in the symbolic forms of animals locked in mortal combat. As Jeff became more comfortable in the group and his story became more apparent through his images, he gradually abandoned his hostile and resistant behaviors. He began to arrive at the sessions early, bringing drawings he'd made at home so he and I could look at them, just the two of us. As his angry distancing maneuvers were cast aside, he allowed himself to become attached to me.

* * * * *

One of the finer attributes of humanity is our resilience in the face of the frightful instability around us. Our capacity to adapt, to change, and to struggle with conflict, both internal and external, is remarkable. A tenet of artistic psychology is that the depth of an individual's existence is determined by how he or she creatively deals with conflict and the anguish it engenders.

The individual's ability to creatively contend with the skirmishes of life marks the difference between a productive, authentic existence and a life marked by defeat and emptiness. This may be described as the capacity for creative resolution.

Longing for Meaning

Many societal trends have contributed to our struggle to attend to events as meaningful experiences. Increased mobility in our society has profoundly altered family life. Relatively few adults live in the hometown of their parents. Divorce, single parenting, and blended families have become common. The past fifty years have brought conspicuous changes in the practice of organized religions. Governmental authority and integrity has been challenged and there is pervasive suspicion regarding the honor of world leaders.

Men and women have lost their foundation, their groundedness. Traditions seem to have lost their meaning, resulting in a generation of ahistorical individuals. Lacking meaningful connections to familial heritage, individuals no longer invest ritual acts with meaning, or have models for culturally based engagement in life. The result is a shallow view of life and a world marked by self-interest and hedonism.

When I have asked people, "What gives your life meaning?" it is disconcerting how often the response is a blank stare, as if I have just spoken in some foreign language. The inability to find meaning in the events of everyday life may be understood as an underlying cause of drug and alcohol abuse, juvenile delinquency, mid-life crises, dysfunctional marriages, and the frequently observed rapid deterioration of those who retire from their life's work.

If we understand *absence of meaning* to be at the core of many of the dysfunctions we experience and see around us in our family and friends, we are left with the problem of what can be done to remedy this absence?

In the context of an artistic psychology the question is how to attend to the emptiness. Obviously, no therapist, no friend, no one outside the self can give meaning to life. How does imagination return to the places it once inhabited? This is a critical question, for if there is no imagination, there is no soul and if there is no soul, there can be no meaning.

Yalom (1980) noted that the dilemma facing us has two propositions that seem unalterably opposed, and yet true.

1. Human beings seem to have need of meaning.
2. Yet, there exists no "meaning," no grand design for the universe, no guidelines for living other than those the individual creates.

At every bend in our lives' paths we are challenged to solve problems and thus uncover the meaning of our lives. Frankl (1969) asserted that "each person is questioned by life; to life he or she can only respond by being responsible." Artistic psychology encourages creation of a personal system of decision making based on the awareness of each person's responsibility to struggle with creating and defining the meaning of his or her life. This cannot be a purely solitary phenomenon. Meaning can be found only in the context of relationships, not in the isolation of the individual psyche. The "me first" attitude so prevalent in Western culture always leaves the individual empty in the end.

Existential emptiness and loss of soul can only be filled through *ensouling experiences,* which can be accomplished only by restoration of the imagination.

CARL'S FEAR

A psychiatrist friend of mine referred Carl to my studio. He was a successful investment broker and a full partner in a distinguished firm. My colleague cautioned me, as we spoke on the telephone about Carl, that this was a frustrating case. I asked why he was referring him to me.

"Bruce, I've been seeing this man in individual therapy for almost three years. He's been in support groups for a long time. He sees a social worker for marital therapy. He's had all this and I don't think he's changed a bit.

"What is troubling him?" I asked.

"Hollowness." The psychiatrist said.

"Hollowness?"

"Hollowness. He seems to function just fine. He managed over twenty million dollars last year. His wife loves him dearly. His kids are nice."

"So what is the problem?" I asked.

"He says his life is worthless."

"What do you think I can do about that?" I wanted to know.

"I'm not sure, but I've just about run out of ideas. Will you see him?"

"Sure, I'll see him."

The next week Carl arrived at the studio. He was a tall man with handsome, chiseled features, deep blue eyes and blonde hair. His voice was a rich bass. He was a good-looking man, but his eyes held a lethargic quality that was discomforting.

He introduced himself and sat on the padded bench opposite my chair. "I feel silly being here."

"Why is that?"

He adjusted his position. "Isn't this really a little childish? I mean, isn't art therapy just for kids?"

"Carl, let's begin by not making presumptions about one another."

He seemed taken aback. "Did I offend . . ."

I interrupted him. "I don't presume that all stock brokers are crooks, though I am sure that some are." He nodded his head in agreement. I asked. "How does feeling childish serve you?"

"It doesn't!"

"Then I advise you to drop it now. Devaluing yourself will not help you here."

He grimaced. "This is preposterous. I don't know what my shrink wants me to get from this?"

"Carl," I said, "I just told you that devaluing yourself will not help in this studio. I assure you that my work is very serious. I see nothing preposterous about it. So, if there is something preposterous, it must be something you brought with you. Calling yourself names will not help."

He sat quietly for a moment. "Okay, let me start over. What is art therapy all about, Mr. Moon?"

"Good. You can call me Bruce, Carl. What did you imagine it would be like?"

"I haven't imagined anything."

"Oh sure you have, Carl. Surely you must have had some picture in your head of what I'd look like, what the studio would be like, and what we'd do today. What did you imagine?"

He ran his fingers through his thick blond hair. "Well, I thought you might look a little like Salvador Dali."

I laughed at that image. "What else?" I asked.

"I don't know what you're asking."

"Did you think that the walls would be any certain color?

"Mm, white I guess. What difference does it make?"

"Close your eyes a moment, Carl. As you thought about coming here, did you imagine any windows in the room? Think back to your fantasy image about coming here. What color did you think the furniture would be?"

"Yes, I did think there would be windows. Modern, slender, wooden frame windows, and skylights. And, I thought the furniture would be plain wood. I don't really know why."

"That's good. You see, Carl, I think we all start out as children able to think in images. Somewhere along the way we forget that and replace our mental pictures with words."

"Does that make a difference?" He wanted to know.

"Carl, have you ever heard the saying that a picture is worth a thousand words?"

"Sure."

"Well, what is it about pictures that would make them worth a thousand words?"

He thought for a moment. "I suppose it's because a picture can say more than words?"

"Exactly," I said. "And there are some pictures that can't be described accurately in words. In fact, most of the really significant experiences in our lives resist verbal description."

"That's why you use images?"

"I don't *use* images, but you are on the right track. I relate to images, not use them."

"How do I get started?" Carl asked.

"Are you sure you want to try this childish therapy?"

"I'm sure I don't want to keep feeling the way I do." He sighed.

"Okay," I said. "Do you dream?"

"I don't think so."

"Well, can you remember any dreams at all?" He sat back on the bench, closed his eyes for a moment.

"There aren't many. But I do remember walking down a hallway, like in an old school. I was naked. That's it."

I handed Carl a piece of paper and a set of colored markers. "I'd like for you to try to draw the hallway you dreamed about."

"I didn't really see it very well."

"I know," I replied. "But try to draw what you think it was like." He drew for the next fifteen minutes or so. The image that emerged was of a long hallway, lined with lockers towering over a naked figure.

His hands shook as he handed me the drawing so that I could see the image. "Yowsa," I exclaimed! "That is a long hall."

"I don't draw well."

"If you meant for the lockers to look immense and frightening, I'd say that you draw very well. Take me into this world, Carl."

"I don't know . . ." He paused.

"Carl, if you could give the lockers a voice, what would they say?"

"I guess they'd . . ."

I interrupted. "No, Carl, give them a voice. Speak as if you were one of the lockers. Tell me about yourself, locker."

"They . . ."

"No, speak from the first person." I demonstrated: "I am this tan locker."

"Okay. I am this locker and I am looking down at this tiny person. I think he's empty, less than empty, really."

"Locker, have you seen this man before?" I asked the image.

"Yes. I've seen him for a long time." Carl's voice lowered. "Not that there's much to look at."

"Locker, how do you feel about this figure?"

Carl laughed disdainfully. "He's good-for-nothing, a con and a humiliation." A few minutes of silence passed as these words hung in the air between Carl and me.

I asked, "Carl, would you give the figure a voice?"

He hesitated. "I am so small. Don't look at me that way." His voice cracked with emotion.

"Whose voice did you hear, Carl, as the locker spoke to you?"

(long pause)

"My mother's. My mother's voice," he wept.

Over the next several sessions, Carl's drawings told the poignant story of his painful relationship with a harsh and distant mother. Carl had never been able to live up to his mother's aspirations for him. She had been unrelentingly derogatory. Carl never could please her.

The hallway Carl drew in our first session together told the story of his feelings of emptiness and desolation. As our relationship developed, the themes of his images shifted from painful issues of unattainable acceptance by his deceased mother to images of faith. Serendipitously he found new meaning in his relationships with his children and his wife. As his feelings about himself changed, he found more creative energy for his work. Carl discovered new purpose as he allowed creativity and imagination to reenter his life.

* * * * *

The search for meaning is central in the lives of all people. Reductionists argue that life can be described as the interrelationship of biological urges. Others suggest that our lives are little more than the collection, row upon row, of habitual patterns of behavior. Therapists who approach their clients from such theoretical foundations regard the search for meaning as a defensive intellectualization or rationalization. As an art therapist, working from an artistic psychological foundation, I do not discount the contributions to our understanding of the human animal that drive theorists and behaviorists have made. However, I do believe there is more to human beings than habit.

The meaning of one's life is one's own. Only the individual can discover it and fulfill it. Yet, in this there exists a paradox that while only the individual can create and fulfill meaning, meaning cannot be found within the individual in isolation. Meaning is always created in the complex interplay of the self and others.

The role of art in the search for meaning is profound. As the artist creates, she struggles with her conscious and unconscious depths to free the image and give it life on the page. The mystery of this process is that the painting reveals not only the obvious reality, but also that which is hidden, that which comes from the distant past and that which is longed for in the future. When the creative activity is finished, the artwork signed and framed, its life, its significance then depends upon the audience. When the artist has allowed the flow of imagery from self to proceed, she has said in her most honest manner, "This is who I am. This is what I am." Whether the artist is a professional, an amateur, or a client, I believe there is a powerful urge to have the artwork be seen by others.

VIOLA'S CLAY FIGURE

The old woman pushed her chair back from the table in the studio. She had just finished polishing a small piece of sculpture. It was a simple, female figure, smooth and sensuous. Resting gently in the middle of the table it evoked a feeling of vulnerability and loneliness. I appreciated the form.

"This is very beautifully done."

Viola replied, "Oh, I don't know."

"I mean it. It's a potent work. It must mean a lot to you."

"No, it's nothing. Just a silly little thing I did."

"Viola, it reminds me of a character in a novel that I read once."

She chuckled, "What?"

"Really. I can't remember the name of the book, but she was the main character. Oh, now I've got it, *The Color Purple*."

Viola replied, "I've heard of the book, but I don't recall the story."

"I'm not real sure I remember much of it either, Viola, but I do remember the main character was a proud and strong woman."

"What does that have to do with this little trinket?"

"You seem strong and proud to me, Viola."

"Is that the truth?" She smiled.

"Well, yes," I said. "I do think it is true. I can see it in your art."

"How?" she wanted to know.

"I'm not sure I can explain. It has something to do with the things artists make."

"What do you mean?" She asked.

"The experiences that hurt or are uncomfortable often are

what motivates artists. I know that I don't make much art when I'm feeling good."

"Why not?"

"I guess I'm too busy feeling good. There's no reason to paint."

Viola asked, "You only paint when you feel bad?"

"Not exactly, but it's something like that."

"And how do you feel after you make things, Bruce?"

"Sometimes I feel better, but sometimes it makes me feel worse."

Viola sighed, "That's the way this is I s'pose." She gently touched the piece with her gnarled hand.

I asked, "It makes you feel sad?"

"Yes, it makes me think of when I was jus' a little thing, down in McComb." (Tears ran down her deeply lined face.)

"It's a beautiful sculpture."

"Thank you."

Artists know that a major reservoir of their creativity is emotional turmoil. One purpose of art at its deepest level is to transform the flaws of life, to take what is painful and ugly and make something with it. This transformation makes sacred the polarities in our lives. It allows the artist to go with the natural flow of life. Nietzsche described healing as an acceptance of conflict and struggle. The creative act is the transforming agent of these powerful forces. It was pleasing to watch Viola in her encounter with the modeling clay. She had come to the hospital following a long period of gradual withdrawl from life. After her husband had died, she had slowly pulled away from everything. At first she handled the clay aimlessly. Then, as the image began to emerge from the clay, her movements became more deliberate and precise. What was initially a vague meandering gradually became a clear encounter between her self, the image, and the clay.

The observable change in her intensity while working was

reflective of a deeper internal process as well. In the beginning she was aimless, noncommittal, and detached. The harder she worked, the more directed she became. The form of the clay figure emerged, speaking eloquently of Viola's sadness and loneliness. Her sculpting was both an external and an internal phenomenon. As she gave form to the clay, she likewise began to mold the emptiness that was within her, to master it. Moving artistic works are born of such inner turmoil and transformation experiences.

Art brings meaning to life by utilizing the raw materials of life, our painful struggles. An artistic psychology understands the central nature of struggle and tension; how the collision of forces brings about the creative process of art. Therapists working from this perspective view their primary task as engendering that same creative attitude towards discomfort in their clients. Through the process of therapy, the client's view of self transforms from that of victim to that of heroine.

Through such transforming experiences the artist is able to affirm her opposites, the parts of herself that are so vulnerable and the parts that are strong enough to persevere. Internal contradictions and conflicts make non-logical sense, as they become the well from which to draw creative inspiration.

We are an amalgam of polarities, contradictions, and inconsistencies. We are engaged in a continual process of change, thus conflict and struggle are inevitable. It is whether or not we are able to accept our evolving, conflicted selves that assures or threatens emotional health. There is a basic tension inside of us that is the manifestation of these polarities. Responses to this tension range from numbness to anxiety to creative resolution. Art does not diminish but instead utilizes the tension in empowering actions. The artist discovers meaning in life as he molds and honors the distressing disharmony of his life. Creation does not ease, but rather ennobles, pain. It does not cure; it accepts. Through the creative actions of art, contradictions and conflicts are brought into sharp focus. Art embraces our deepest fears, loneliness, pain, and guilt. As the artist works, he collides with pieces of self that are often distasteful and sometimes disturbing. On occasion the discoveries are pleasant, even noble.

Most often, the artistic expressions of my clients are awkward, frightening, and raw. As the therapist, my task is to invite these painful expressions into the therapeutic relationship, as if they were guests. I provide an atmosphere of welcome and empathy that encourages the heroic effort required of clients to confront aspects of themselves they find disturbing or distressing. The work of an art therapist is to accompany clients as they explore, create, and uncover the meanings of their lives.

TOM BROWN AND GRAY

Tom didn't feel like talking. He simply no longer had the desire to speak. He was the victim of years of sadistic physical abuse. He had little left to say.

When he was referred to my art therapy group I wondered how he would fit in. During the first session, as I explained the purposes and structure of the group, Tom made momentary eye contact with me but quickly looked away. "Tom, this is a group where we use drawing as a way of expressing and sharing feelings. You don't have to be Picasso or DaVinci or anybody like that. Whatever you draw will be ok. I promise you that in this group I will always take your feelings seriously. Welcome, I'm glad you are here."

The opening ritual of the group was to sit in a circle and for each member, in a word or two, to share the feeling he or she was bringing to the session on that day. As it came to Tom's turn he looked down at the floor, pulled his arms against his body, leaned forward in his chair, but said nothing.

To the group members I said, "Today, I want us to imagine a room, any room. When an image comes, try to draw what you see."

It was customary for the group members to work with colored chalk on large sheets of brown craft paper taped to the wall. Tom immediately moved to a place at the wall and began to draw. He covered his paper with solid brown. Then he used a light gray pastel to sketch a rough picture of an empty room. The room had a dark ceiling, a wooden door, and a window with sheer curtains. In one corner a small figure stood against the walls. When it was his turn to talk about his image Tom shook his head and looked down at the floor.

Many of Tom's art group sessions went like this. He rarely said more than a few words at a time. Instead, he drew places, people, and events from his life. He always used brown and gray. Sometimes his pictures were disturbing, and sometimes too confusing for me to understand. I believe that by making pictures of these places and events Tom was able to face his fears and find meaning in the awful events of his past. He gave time and attention to people and places through his creative work. His pictures were often of the people who had treated him so horribly. He drew places where the inhumane crimes against him had been perpetrated. Yet, they became more than that, for Tom used his ability to create, to picture himself in a position of power. He was the creator of his drawings, and through this he created the meaning of his story. He ennobled his position and shifted from being the victim to being the hero of his image-stories. He resolved many of his inner conflicts and created meaning through his creative work.

On one day, not long before he was discharged, Tom drew a picture of a monster that seemed to be attacking a tiny, quivering boy. When it was his turn to talk about his drawing, Tom quietly said, "I will tame this monster. That's what this has all been about, hasn't it?" This led other group members into a poignant discussion of our human nature, our capacity for being both villain and hero.

In the safety of the studio, meaning is created as images of pain, fear, and courage are *arted out*. The making of images opens us to the mystery that is within each person.

Perhaps there are some therapists who would say my description of Tom's pictures as an example of the creation of meaning is purely speculative fiction. But, I was there. I saw him use his imagination, create artworks, and make meaning in his life.

Figure 4. Making art is a way of reflecting upon the mythological aspects of everyday life.

Chapter III

ART AS SPIRITUAL PRACTICE

There are two ways of thinking about church and religion. One is that we go to church in order to be in the presence of the holy, to learn and to have our lives influenced by that presence. The other is that church leads us directly and symbolically to see the sacred dimension of everyday life. (Moore, 1992, p. 214)

Art making as a spiritual practice is a kind of spirituality that is both ordinary and extraordinary. It is a way of reflecting upon the mythological aspects of everyday life, the sacred stories that give fictional form to the essential truths of human existence. Artistic images are manifestations of the ordinary and the mythic that emerge from interactions among artist, media, and mythic themes. The spiritual qualities associated with words like *manifestation* and *myth* are helpful in describing how images emerge because these words suggest that images come from a deeper source than the artist's technical skills.

I am intrigued by the idea that as I paint, I pray. Prayer is "the act or practice of praying, as to God; an earnest request; an utterance in praise, adoration, confession, supplication and thanksgiving, etc.; any spiritual communion, as with God" (Webster, p. 1060).

Regardless of the form of one's faith–faith in God, or gods, or life itself–it is reflected in the art we make. As an artist therapist, I regard the therapeutic journey as a sacred quest my clients and I undertake. The primary mode of our communicative travels is the images we create, the visual prayers of the pilgrimage. In the sanctuary of the studio, confessions are drawn, thanksgivings painted, and praises framed. It is a holy thing we do, this making art and healing wounds.

Art making is a spiritual practice for me, but it is quite different from the spirituality often associated with organized religion. McNiff (1989) notes that, "where religions focus on prophets from the past, art suggests that we are all prophets in potentiality" (p. 16). The artist's form of spirituality is connected to the human longing to be in contact with soul, the source of meaning in life. The spiritual aspect of art making pays attention to the experience of awe and wonder at the world around us. The interplay of art and spirituality is an expression of our deep yearning for soulful life.

If we believe that God is revealed in scriptures, then the primary image we have of God is as creator. "The artist comes closer to 'The Creator' through participation in the process of creation in art" (McNiff, 1989, p. 22). It is consistent for those who seek a life close to God to involve themselves in creative work.

Images and imagination serve to give form to raw, incomprehensible and mythic themes of everyday life. Art making involves the transformation of inner images into external forms. The spiritual practice of making art requires the courage to pay attention to and give form to imagination's themes. The poet, the painter, the musician, and the dancer all operate from guiding inner visions and all work to give these visions form.

As I approach my canvas, the possibilities are endless. Anything might appear on that pristine surface. My encounter with the empty canvas is not unlike that of the writer, Stephen King, who in his novel, *Misery,* eloquently describes the hole that appears in the blank page of typing paper. As it gradually opens, the story unfolds in his imagination (1988).

It is similar for me as I stand before the empty canvas. I never know beforehand exactly what will come. I sit and look and ever so gradually the image presents itself. At the height of my creative work, it sometimes seems as if there is an image-orator and I am little more than a stenographer. In these times, I become engrossed in an imaginal inner existence. This encounter may best be described as creative immersion.

The spiritual practice of creative immersion may serve to clarify the difference between a talented craftsperson and an authentic artist. When I taught at the Columbus College of Art and Design, I came into contact with many gifted craftspersons enrolled in the schools of industrial design or commercial art. While their activity yielded products of technical brilliance, their work often lacked the passion and soul of the fine arts students' work. The critical difference between these two groups of students was that the industrial designers and commercial artists made things on demand to meet external criteria of acceptability to the client while the fine arts students engaged in the process of creative immersion.

Some time ago, I worked with a young man in the hospital art studio. One day, upon entering the room, he immediately gathered paints and odd scraps of canvas. He hurriedly taped the canvas scraps together, creating a patchwork surface approximately 3′ x 3′ square. I asked him if he was going to gesso this uncommon surface. He shook his head and said, "No, I don't have time."

There was something in his eyes that accentuated his sense of urgency. I usually insist that canvases be built and prepared correctly, but the look in his eyes led me to forego my customary expectations.

He dove into his work with both hands. He smeared, pushed, and layered the acrylic paint. After an hour of work he stepped away from a thickly textured, disturbingly dark and brooding image of a human face.

After the session, one of my students questioned me as to why I allowed the young man to "waste paint."

My response was, "I don't know why I did that. It just seemed to make sense."

The young artist returned to the studio only one time after that session. He came to pick up his painting. As he was leaving he turned back to me and said, "Thanks."

In retrospect, I am convinced that his creative immersion pushed me to behave in a manner uncommon for me. The young man's painting was disturbing, but it was genuine.

What I am describing here, this spiritual practice of art making, is essentially an involvement between the artist, media, imagination, and the world. It is this involvement that illustrates Hillman's (1989) definition of soul as that which turns random events into meaningful experiences.

The artistic dimension of spirituality involves the mystery of the creative interaction among artist, media, imagination, and the world. Art making is an act of love that is neither earned nor imposed. In describing the poetic dimension of religion, McNiff (1989) says, "It embodies love, healing, mystery, divine expression and human attempts to become involved in creation" (p. 22). One may think of creation and making as acts of grace. They cannot be forced, and they are not deserved. They simply happen. The mystery is felt as the artist steps back from her sculpture in order to gain a different perspective. It is sensed as people pause in passing to take in the meaning of the form. The mystery is felt as the artist signs the work, knowing that her name does more than signify, "I did this." Rather it proclaims, "I am this!"

Frankl (1959) wrote that love does not make us blind, it lets us see. All images and objects are embraced and given meaning through the grace of love. From meaning comes the motivation to create again. This establishes a cyclical process.

From creation comes meaning, from meaning comes motivation, from motivation comes creation, and on and on the cycle spins.

Fromm (1956) suggested that for love to exist there must be five human elements present. They are: discipline, concentration, patience, mastery, and faith (pp. 97–120). I submit these same conditions must be present in the spiritual practice of art making. The relationship among artist, media, imagination, and the world is utterly tied to the presence of discipline, concentration, patience, mastery, and faith.

Discipline

Engaging in the spiritual practice of art processes requires discipline. We can never be good, truly good, at anything if our efforts are undisciplined. This, of course, implies practice, repetition, and struggle. When I lead workshops, I ask participants to work with the same image over several hours. Students, therapists, and artists alike often find this a difficult task. They lament that it would be much easier to work on several images rather than to stay with the same one for such an extended period. My response is to gently redirect them to their work. "There is always more that you can do . . . there is always a deeper level that the image wants to take you to."

I do not take their struggle lightly. I know it requires discipline to stick with the work, especially when it is not going well, or when it seems as if one has done all that can be done. I know this is hard work. Still, I insist they keep working with the same image. This sets the stage for all that follows.

Anything we try to do only when we are in the mood for it may be amusing or it may pass the time, but it is not art. This presents a difficulty in our culture, for, in large part, we have lost our appreciation for self-discipline. Confounding the problem is the fact that discipline must pervade the artist's entire existence. Our culture, however, seems to deify avoidance and escape. Time off, time away from the rigors of work has been glorified. We have developed into a society displaying precious little self-discipline. It has been argued that the symptoms of this communal flaw are evident in a variety of sociological phenomena such as drug and alcohol abuse, domestic violence, and dysfunctional families. Without self-discipline, life is random and chaotic, what Frankl describes as the "existential vacuum" (p. 128).

In the arts studios where I have worked, the tone for disciplined engagement with the arts is set in many subtle ways. Easiest to describe is the approach to the task of painting. I use no pre-stretched, pre-gessoed, or factory constructed canvases. During my first encounters with clients I encourage an authentic and active engagement with materials and processes. Rather than provide the client with a readymade canvas upon which to paint, I begin the therapeutic journey by engaging the client in using a miter saw to cut canvas stretchers from 2 x 2s and constructing the frame. The client and I work together to brace and nail the frame, and stretch and staple the canvas. Applying gesso correctly is the final step in the disciplined process of preparing to paint. This approach establishes a model of authentic engagement with materials, tools, and procedures, which becomes an important aspect of the clients' struggle with creative expression. This struggle is metaphoric of the intense self-discipline that clients must apply to other aspects of their lives. If clients are to find (or make) genuine meaning out of the random chaos of their lives, it is critical that they exert control. Without discipline, there can be no art. Without discipline, there can be no focused concentration.

Concentration

In addition to discipline, the spiritual practice of art also requires the ability to focus. Concentration is an essential element for true engagement in art. Everyone who has ever tried to learn to dance, play the piano, or struggle with oil paints knows the capacity for concentration is critical. Yet, even more than discipline, focus seems to be an endangered species in our world today. So many things go on all at once. In the span of a twenty minute drive to work, I can listen to the radio, talk to my wife, yell at the driver in front of me, think about the day ahead, remember the basketball game from the night before, be aware of traffic signs, and watch out for the moves of other drivers.

Our culture is sometimes viewed as a monstrous, open-mouthed consumer. We have become so accustomed to visual stimulation that movies and television shows seldom allow an image to remain constant on the screen for more than a few seconds. The use of fleeting imagery has been taken to new levels by music videos. Political campaigns use momentary visual images mixed with sound bites to create impressions of candidates while offering little solid information concerning candidates' views on critical issues of the day. We indiscriminately consume visual stimulation.

To be still, without talking, smoking, drinking, or doing something is nearly impossible for many people. Yet without focus there can be no art.

In the therapeutic arts studio, the therapist can be thought of as an artist-in-residence. The artist-in-residence becomes the shepherd of the studio atmosphere, maintaining a healthy, disciplined, and focused studio. At the same time, the atmosphere of the studio must not be overly regimented, for that is the antithesis of spontaneity and creativity.

In my work with emotionally disturbed adolescents, playing music is an environmental element that requires vigilant attention. The radio is an integral cultural phenomenon for adolescents. At times, having the radio on provides an invaluable connecting point between the client and me. Rock and roll music has primitive rhythms and potent lyrics that stir our internal creative forces, but music can set the tone in the studio in both positive and negative ways. Sometimes the lyrics, or what is known about a musician's life, provide a common ground on which to initiate dialogue and begin relationships. In other instances, the adolescents may turn the stereo volume so high that conversation is made difficult, thus impeding relationship formation. There are other times when a particular song lyric may be inappropriate for a therapeutic studio setting. I have no misgivings about occasionally censoring the music in the therapeutic studio.

As an artist therapist my first responsibility is to maintain a safe and predictable therapeutic milieu in the studio. The inclusion of music in the environment is at times healthy and appropriate, at other times detrimental. There are no set rules or formulas for these issues, but one must be vigilant about all aspects of the arts milieu, continually assessing whether the studio is safe, predictable, and comfortable. If it is not, concentration on tasks will be difficult to maintain, for both client and therapist. If there is no focus, there can be no art.

Patience

The spiritual practice of art also requires patience. If you have ever tried to work with clay on the potter's wheel, you know very well that nothing is achieved without patience. Learning to throw on the wheel takes time, so much time. It takes time to wedge the clay properly in order to remove all the air bubbles. It takes time to master the process of centering. One must patiently try and try, and try again to insert the thumbs properly in order to open the clay. It takes time to perfect pulling the clay upward. If you attempt to hurry, or take a shortcut through any one of these steps, the piece is ruined.

In contemporary times, patience is as difficult as discipline and focus. Our way of life fosters and rewards quick results. Computers are machines revered for their speed. In an instant, they can give their users access to information and research data that would have taken weeks of intensive labor just a few years ago. However, speed is not of the essence when it comes to imagining and making. In fact, doing these things quickly may be the antithesis of doing them well.

In my work, one of the most challenging tasks is helping clients learn to slow down. The arts provide a powerful action metaphor for this aspect of the client's treatment. Artistic processes simply cannot be hurried. For example, the raw canvas must be covered with gesso. The gesso must be allowed at least a few hours to dry thoroughly before the next phase of the painting process can proceed. Clients are often frustrated with this aspect of their work in the creative arts studio. I try never to miss these opportunities to comment on the nature of the arts, therapy, and life itself.

I respond to my impatient client, "Lisa, you're going to have to let the gesso dry for the rest of this session. Why don't you use the time to think about what you are going to paint? Or you might want to make some sketches to plan your painting."

Lisa says, "But I want to paint today."

"I understand, but some things just take time, you can't hurry this or you'll make a mess of things."

Lisa replies, "Can't I start as soon as the gesso is mostly dry?"

"No, you really have to wait until it's completely dry. The canvas will be entirely sealed then and will hold the colors better."

"But I really thought I'd get to start painting today. I don't want to think about it anymore and I don't like to plan. I want to paint."

I respond, "It's important to take your time. Be patient."

"I don't like being patient. I want to paint now."

"Well, Lisa, in art it just doesn't work that way. You have to cooperate with the materials and procedures. That's sort of like life you know."

Lisa complains, "I'm' getting bored."
"Do you know where boredom comes from?" I ask.
"What are you talking about?"
"You said you were bored. I think that boredom comes from an absence of quality relationships. If you have good relationships in your life, it doesn't matter where you are, or what you are doing, you are never bored. On the other hand, if you don't have quality relationships, you could be at Disney World and be bored. Do you see what I mean?"

Unconvinced, Lisa says, "What's that got to do with art?"
"Well, good relationships take time to grow. You have to be patient with them; they can't be hurried. It's the same with making art. You can't make the gesso dry faster than it will. You have to be patient."

Mastery

If one has discipline, focus, and patience, then mastery of tasks and materials is possible. In the spiritual practice of art, the artist must be concerned with mastery of the task. If the art, if the imagining, is not of ultimate concern, the beginner can never really make art. One may be a dabbler or hobbyist but never really an artist. I regard it as crucial that my students and clients learn to draw, shade, drybrush, layer, and wash. In so doing, they experience themselves as being capable of slowing down, rethinking, and struggling with the process. There is no magic that determines one person is an artist and another is not. The only genuine route to mastery is practice.

Unfortunately, many people in our time have lost touch with the ability to struggle. Many people I have met lament that they cannot paint. I mourn the fact that they do not struggle or practice. Rather, they give in to the frustration of "failed" efforts and avoid the pain of future inadequacy by giving up the activity. Nothing valuable or meaningful comes conveniently or easily. An artistic psychology embraces the notion that all of us must reclaim our identity as artists who are ultimately concerned with both process and product.

STEPHANIE'S BLOOD AND TEARS

Stephanie entered the studio hesitantly. She was accompanied by one of the attendants from the adolescent unit. Although she said nothing about being individually accompanied due to her suicidality, there was an air of deep resentment that seemed to ooze from her pores. It was cold that day and as she took off her coat, I saw that both of her arms were wrapped in gauze from wrist to elbow. There were small bloodstains discoloring the sterile bandages.

"Welcome to the studio, Stephanie. My name is Bruce. I am an artist. What we do here is work with the images inside us. Take a look around at the work other people are doing. I'll touch base with you in a few minutes and we'll get you started making something."

She said nothing, but her eyes quickly took in the room. I was working at my easel when Stephanie approached. "I think I'd like to paint," She said, with a sense of urgency in her voice. We built a canvas together.

The next day Stephanie began to work immediately. She mixed a deep burgundy and covered the entire canvas with the dark, rich color. She then used a brighter, more intense red to paint the shape of a large heart. A black dagger was portrayed penetrating the top of the heart. She then added dark, midnight blue teardrops falling from the wound. All of this happened in a little less than an hour.

The next afternoon, when she returned to the studio, she placed her painting on an easel, stepped back a few feet and sighed disgustedly, "Damn, this isn't right."

"Stephanie," I said, "it's a powerful piece. What is bothering you about it?"

"Oh, I'm not exactly sure. But when I step back it all just

seems so dark. I mean you can see the heart, but almost every-thing else seems to get lost in the dark red."

I stood beside her. "I see what you mean. Do you mind a suggestion?" She shook he head, no. "Well, if I was you, I think I'd work on the teardrops some more. You might try mixing your midnight blue again and then add some white to it. I think that if you highlight the right side of each tear, and blend the light blue gradually into the dark, it will make the tears really stand out against the background."

She sighed again. "I don't know how to do that. I better just leave it the way it is."

"Stephanie, trust me, I'm an expert at this. Try what I am suggesting. If you don't like it, you can always paint over it again. But don't give up without even trying."

After the session, one of my graduate students told me she was dismayed by my apparent aesthetic judgments of Stephanie's image. She angrily said, "You should have just ac-cepted whatever Stephanie did and not offered any technical advice."

I responded, "I think it's my obligation to help Stephanie become a more skilled artist. Think of it this way, you don't express yourself verbally today in the same way you did when you were four years old. You have been taught how to articu-late your ideas. Your vocabulary has expanded and you've learned how to express your thoughts in a sophisticated way. The same thing can be true in art. Of course, Stephanie's work was acceptable, but she can make it even more effec-tive by learning new techniques . . . expanding her artistic vocabulary."

The following day, Stephanie highlighted the tears. They seemed to come alive on the board. She asked, "Could I do something like that to the heart and the dagger?"

"Sure," I said, "the concept is simple. Your light on the tears is coming from the right side, so just add touches of light to the right side of the heart and the dagger blade."

Stephanie did not say too much about what these images meant to her. But she did hold the painting close to her as she carried it out later that week. It was as if she was cradling an infant, protecting it . . . caring for it. Perhaps that is exactly what she was doing.

* * * * *

Faith

In the spiritual practice of art, each of these four elements–discipline, concentration, patience and mastery–depend utterly upon the necessary element of *Faith*. Involvement in art, imagining and making, demands faith. By this I mean faith in the goodness of life, in the arts, in others, and in ourselves. Fromm (1956) said, ". . . only the person who has faith in himself is able to be faithful to others" (p. 111).

My faith in imagery has been strengthened through many experiences with art and with living. Artists show us portraits of ourselves as we really are and artistic psychology suggests that the primary task of art is to engage people in imaginal dialogues about the way life is. No disguises are necessary.

As an active artist, my work sometimes soothes me, while at other times, it torments me. Sometimes I look at my paintings and I am awestruck by the strength and goodness I see. At other times, I am terrified by the wounded, haunted, weakness I see. Yet I have faith in the process.

Sometimes life presents us with experiences that are utterly unbearable, and yet somehow they must be endured. Late in May of 1995, I entered my house and heard a voice leaving a message on our telephone answering machine. Although I did not hear the exact words, I could tell by the tone of the voice that something awful had happened. I hurried to pick up the phone. The person on the other end told me friends of our family, Debbie DeBrular and her husband Bo Orahood, had been killed in an airplane crash. Debbie was my wife's closest friend. Years before, she had been one of my graduate students and over the course of fifteen years had become a respected colleague.

Bo had recently earned his pilots' license. He'd flown Debbie, their nine-year-old daughter, Molly, and one of Molly's friends to a family reunion in West Virginia. They crashed in a failed attempt at landing. What really happened may never be known for sure.

As I stood listening to this horrible news, Cathy approached me. She could tell that something was wrong. When I hung up the phone I said, "Cathy, you'd better sit down, I have some terrible news. She sat and I broke the news. "Debbie and Bo have been killed in a plane accident."

I remember wanting somehow to protect Cathy from the pain I knew would come. It was difficult to believe; Debbie and Bo simply could not be dead. The sorrow of late May stayed with me a long time. It forced me to deal with the reality that I too could die without warning. It reminded me that I have little control over my life, really. The world does not revolve around my schedule or my wishes.

Not long after the plane crash, I made a painting of a woman sitting alone in a diner. She is smoking a cigarette. She appears lost in thought. The painting wasn't intended to be any particular woman. I thought at first that it might be a symbolic portrait of isolation and fear, but it's more than that. It captures the essence of several painful losses in my life. I recognize the look in her eyes. When I finished it, I stood in my studio and cried. The woman in the painting looks sad, as if she has so much left to do. And she seems frightened, aware of what she does not control. She reminds me of the way my life is. In the deepest sense, she is a portrait of me.

Imagining and making are sacred tasks. Every time I dip my woundedness in pigment or dust it with chalk, I nourish myself. Making art gives me the courage I need to continue on life's journey. Making art is powerful and good.

I have deep faith in this powerful goodness. The image is always more than I thought it would be, bigger than I expected and more powerful than I ever dreamed. The image of the woman in the diner came from the interplay among the paint, the mythic/everyday theme of loss, and myself. As I paint, I pray, "God, help me."

Spirituality is practiced in the art we make. In the sanctuary of the studio, I confess, give thanks, and praise. Making art is a holy thing to do.

* * * * *

In contemporary times, it is no longer necessary for people to use their creativity. Creativity is seen as the private attribute of the artist, entertainer, or scientist. We seldom speak of the creative potential of the average person. Those who define themselves as creative all too often indulge in self-aggrandizing elitism, excluding the common person from the ranks of the creative. The severity of such an error is not only that the "creative people" delude themselves, but also that frequently the world at large accepts the delusion.

Art history teaches that the truly lasting works of great art are those that inspire us to wrestle with the confounding themes of existence. Humanity's relation to God, nature, war, sexuality, society, and self are among the motifs repeated time and again. From the prehistoric cave paintings of France, to Michelangelo's *Sistine Chapel,* to Picasso's *Guernica,* to Dali's *Last Supper,* over and over the scenes are those of humankind's struggle to interpret existence, to make contact with soul.

A hallmark of emotional and mental health is the ability to contend with the struggle and anguish of life. Persons who come to therapy are often those who are in conflict. They have been unable to successfully cope, fully defend, or satisfactorily adapt. Their lives bear the scars of having been beaten and battered by their struggle with life.

Artistic psychology calls upon the inherent creative potential of every person. Creativity is enlisted as an ally in the complicated task of unraveling the tangled strands of life, freeing the person from the snare of victimization. Commenting on this capacity of art, Levine writes, "The use of the arts as a means of healing the soul testifies to the inherent power of men and women to confront the depths of their own pain and to emerge with a sense that life is indeed worth living" (pp. 6–7).

The primary task of art therapists is doing creative work with the arts in the service of client well being. By so doing, they call out the creative potential of clients. As artists, we know that conflict is inherent in painting, sculpting, molding, dancing, and making. By virtue of all that has been created in the name of art, we stand at a pivotal point in the acceptance and expression of conflict. Making art is a natural method of expressing and responding to the energies of soul. Making art is a means of evoking and sharing feelings and ideas that are essentially conflictive and sometimes disturbing. An artistic psychology is based in the belief that people are capable of creative resolution of problems in artistic work and this capacity can be applied to other areas of life.

Artistic psychology does not encourage focusing attention on one specific conflict, but rather on the nature of conflict as a symbol of life in process. If this attitude can be engendered, then particular struggles will no longer be avoided, but rather will be embraced as a validation of life itself.

Art comes from the depths of human experiences. Born of passion, discord, fear, and courage, art processes make meaning visible by transforming events. It is in the moments of our lives when casual events are turned into meaning-filled experiences that soul is most present (Hillman, 1989). Making art can be a spiritual practice, a process of *ensoulment*.

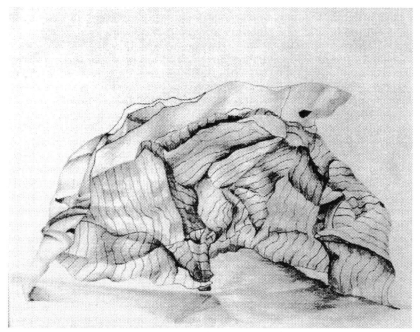

Figure 5. Art involves the use of skill (craftsmanship) and creative imagination in the production of objects or events to convey a fundamental quality of life as it is.

Chapter IV

ART

W hat is art?
 The *American Heritage Dictionary of the English Language* (1978) defines art as "the conscious production or arrangement of sounds, colors, forms, movements, or other elements in a manner that affects the sense of beauty; specifically, the production of the beautiful in a graphic or plastic medium" (p. 74). Art historian H. W. Janson (1973) wrote, "the creative process consists of a long series of leaps of the imagination and the artist's attempts to give them form by shaping the material accordingly" (p. 10).

Science, technology, and philosophy significantly influence the spiritual condition of a particular time. These influences can be either constructive or destructive in nature. Paul Tillich (1965) wrote, "Art indicates what the character of a spiritual situation is; it does this more immediately and directly than do science and philosophy for it is less burdened by objective considerations" (p. 85). In contrast to science, which always must contend with observable data, art can serve as a mediator among objective considerations, subjective experiences, and intuitive impressions. In a sense, an important task of art is to be more concerned with exploring and expressing meaning than understanding substance.

Since the beginning of the twentieth century, the emptiness and loss of soul in Western society has often been directly expressed in painting. The artistic movements of expressionism, impressionism, surrealism, abstraction, minimalism, and the more recent artistic trends of performance art and public art arguably could be regarded as rebellious creative reactions against utilitarianism, hedonism, and the resulting existential emptiness. One primary aspect of each of these movements is that they expose, explore, and express communal meanings while simultaneously creating personal meaning for the individual artist.

For my purposes in this text, I refer often to the *arts*. By this, I mean painting, sculpture, drawing, poetry, music, dance, and drama. I do not include the *crafts*. I must note here that I am aware that this is clearly a modernist view of art. While I am interested in postmodern ideas regarding art, I am most familiar with the modernist position. This is not to disparage craftsmanship, for I have the highest regard for skillful handling of materials, but I distinguish craft from art. Without denigrating the masterful manipulation of materials (craft), I think art involves the intent to express some essential aspect of human existence. "Whereas the craftsman only attempts what he knows to be possible, the artist is always driven to attempt the impossible—or at least the improbable" (Janson, p. 12). Art involves the use of skill (craftsmanship) and creative imagination in the production of objects or events to convey a fundamental quality of life as it is. Originality and intent distinguishes art from craft. Many artists begin at the level of craftsmanship, learning techniques, copying other artists' styles and becoming familiar with the control of media. Through this, the artist-to-be assimilates the artistic tradition. The artistic heritage is the common ground between the individual artist and the world. Just as familial traditions provide children with a root system from which to grow, so too artistic tradition provides each artist with a foundation upon which to build.

Just what art is, and differentiating good art from bad, has been the source of argument and controversy for as long as there have been artists, and certainly for as long as there have been art critics. Defining art has been a bit like holding mercury, a slippery and elusive task. The subtle ambiguity and indescribability of the word "art" derives from the unclear and complicated standing of art itself in our culture. Some artists' works are regarded as being of great value. Some artists' works are discounted as worthless. Art can be regarded simultaneously as frivolous and important, powerful and impotent, sublime and pornographic, religious and secular. How confusing!

Some regard the products of art as having a life of their own, entities unto themselves. Others argue that artworks are nothing more than decorations or frills. Art seems to have no single, fixed, agreed upon definition. I have associated art with love, structure, chaos, play, work, communication, hope, mastery, benevolence (Moon, 1994). I have described art making as emotional, sensual, comforting, and afflicting (Moon, 1995). Thus, just what art is would seem to depend heavily upon the given circumstances from which it comes. Perhaps we can best say art is paradoxical by nature, at various times involving all these attributes and more.

A prominent characteristic of imagery as I think of it is that it is inextricably woven into the fabric of daily life. So tight is the weave, it is difficult to separate for the purpose of exploration. Images are a part of the fabric of human existence. We encounter imagery in various forms every day in our work places, in advertisements, magazine covers, television shows, movies, and in the places we live. We cannot escape them!

In this book, I refer to art activities as those creative, intentional involvements with materials for expressive purposes. The expressive focus may be personal, communal, or both. It is the intention to express that sets art apart from craft and craftsmanship. In the artistic psychology I am proposing, a primary aim of art making is to restore the individual (or corporate) soul by reestablishing image as the foundation of life. As a therapist, my intention is to aid the artist client in knowing him or herself in a deeper way. In artistic psychology, deepening the artist's self-understanding and mindfulness is the ultimate goal of art making. Healing, in an artistic psychology, is a process of soul restoration.

From the viewpoint of the artist, images and their messages are emerging stories that have no final chapter. Artistic engagement is never-ending because the story enters into death and death is limitless. In an artistic psychology creative healing transforms life into death and transcends death into life through creative activity. In the realm of imagination, knowing the self is continual because it has no connection to time. Mindfulness evolves. Yalom (1995) describes mindfulness as being aware of one's self-creation: ". . . the authentic state of mindfulness of being provides one with the power to change" (p. 94). Achieving mindfulness through art making is revelatory, circular, disjointed; it is like music, sometimes harmonious, sometimes dissonant, sometimes rhythmic, sometimes syncopated. Every artistic endeavor has its own beginning, middle, and end. Self-understanding is made possible by active work with images and imagination. There is no other end than the act of reclamation of imagination itself, which is in effect an act of soul restoration. When one acts in this manner, whether consciously or unconsciously, one is making art, which is making soul.

Art affects people by revealing ever-present meanings that deepen, enrich and ensoul their experience of daily life. Art involves construction, ownership, and sharing with others the complex arrangement of how the world and individual lives are perceived. Art promotes awareness and embrace of life as it is. It provides opportunities for validation from, and attachment to, others. Art transcends the individual while simultaneously deepening and defining the individual. Art celebrates the mundane and the amazing, the routine and the extraordinary aspects of existence.

In her ethological study, *What Is Art For,* Dissanayake (1988) draws to an end with, "I will venture to conclude, however, that what the arts were for, an embodiment and reinforcement of socially shared significances, is what we crave and are perishing for today" (p. 200). Throughout history the arts have always served the same critical needs they serve today.

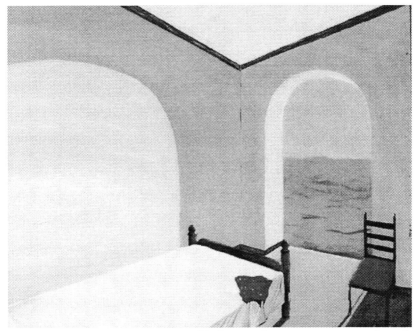

Figure 6. By making art, we give visible form to the imaginative interplay of external experience and internal meaning, and thus create structure in our encounters with life.

Chapter V

IMAGE

The arts serve as the meeting ground of outer and inner vision. With outer vision, the artist explores the world around her; with inner vision, she explores herself. Both worlds, external and internal, are filled with sensual experiences: tactile, olfactory, visual, auditory, and kinesthetic. The internal realm is molded by the traces left in our systems of visual encounters with the external world. These visual experiences form images that construct dreams, embody emotions, organize sensations, and ascribe meaning to experiences. Without such images our memories would be incoherent and meaningless and our experiences would be random and irrational.

By making art, we give visible form to the imaginative interplay of external experience and internal meaning, and thus create structure in our encounters with life. These images come in the forms of paintings, drawings, sculptures, poems, dances, and songs and are primary modes of communication. Formed images move from the realm of the maker's individual experiences into the arena of the community's shared experiences. The interaction between the individual and the community is one of the foundational elements of an artistic psychology.

The image is an essential message to and from one's emotions, intellect, senses, and soul. The messages of art are delivered to one's entirety simultaneously. Throughout history, people have turned to images to keep them apprised of the world around them, to tell them about life on the grand scale and how they fit into the larger scheme of things. Artistic imagery has assisted the process of balancing outer and inner experiences and has provided a mechanism for producing internal images of external phenomena. These inner portraits of life are formed with pathos toward the triumphs and tragedies, hopes and fears, and pleasures and pains of the individual. Even more important, artworks have given humankind a perception that there is order amidst the chaos of existence. In this sense images, and the artworks that emerge from them, are the center of experience, the foundation of feeling and thought.

An essential aspect of artistic expression is that it brings inner and outer vision into compatible form. Artistic imagery expresses through the structure of its form. The structure is distinct. Shape, line, and color are organized in such a way as to become metaphoric of the feelings and ideas the artist meant to express, as well as those she did not intend. Thus, artistic images are more than a reporting of sensual experience, more than definition of emotional reaction, and more than a charting of thoughts. An artwork has meaning at all of these levels. Images are an expressive form created directly from sensation, but extending far beyond sensation, integrating and connecting all the levels of inner life, emotion, thought, and soul. The fundamental union of external and internal experience makes artistic images a uniquely human phenomenon.

It is the union of feeling, thought, sensation, and soul in artistic images that forms art's exceptional contributions to the larger human culture as well as to the individual person. The meaning and depth of artistic expression is made poorer if any one of these four qualities is left out or given undo representation. It is upon the foundation of understanding the arts

as a union of feeling, thought, sensation, and soul that the notion of art as a psychotherapeutic process is built.

Levine (1992) notes, "Art gives voice to suffering. It expresses the pain and confusion of the disintegration of the self,
and, in so doing, enables clients to face themselves without
reservation" (p. 23). When an artist paints an image of suffering, or creates a dance of anguish, she gives herself up to her
suffering and anguish. In the creative artistic moment, images
of wholeness may emerge that embody the possible resolution of the distress. By giving the artist an opportunity to express suffering, the arts offer the possibility of transcending
suffering. "Art then can be both a cry of despair in the night as
well as a triumphant hosanna of joy" (Levine, p. 23).

An artwork that comes from a purely intellectual appraisal
of the environment, without emotion or enthusiasm, is nothing more than an empty illustration. Likewise, artistic images
that only serve the purpose of cathartic expression of feeling,
without any sense of connection to the world outside the individual, are little more than graphic depictions of temporary
emotion. Color, form, shape, and line have no genuine impact
upon us if they do not grow out of thoughtful, sensual, and
passionate involvement in life. Images created without engagement of thought, sensation, and emotion are often frag-
mentary and devoid of meaning.

Images lay bare the assumptions of their makers. If the
artist's vision is sensitive, her images will become our own.
They will teach us about our selves and the world. Images
emerge from our existence, for our existence. The things we
think about, the things we feel and the sensations we experience form the basis of our capacity to transform a world of
chaos into one of order.

The hard, mechanical rhythm of the industrial west has
given way to the click of the microchip. Information, measured in megabytes, has become the symptomatic product of
our time. Artistic imagination can teach us again to unite all

levels of our experience. The technological revolution, symbolized by the in-home personal computer, has led to the dulling of the best qualities of human creativity. The absence of depth, color, and light, and the insipidness of mass entertainment are as malevolently infectious to the soul as acid rain is to the forest, or carbon monoxide to the air we breathe. Artistic psychology urges us to use our faculties to the fullest; the sculptor's hands, the painter's eyes, the poet's words, the singer's voice—the artist's soul.

Imagicide

We run the risk of killing off the imagination whenever we attempt to label or analyze its products, or demand to know what they mean. When we attempt to intellectually describe the meaning of an image, we are essentially trying to translate it into an idea or concept we are able to understand, one with which we are comfortable. The drawing of a cave (Figure 7) cannot be explained as the wish to return to the womb, as an expression of unmet dependency needs, or as a representation of sexual fantasies without ignoring the cave itself. The effort to reductively interpret, and label or classify images is fundamentally an attempt to commit image-murder. Few people go to an art gallery or concert hall for the sake of being told what the paintings or the music means. Instead, they go for the sake of using their own imagination, to discover meanings for themselves. Narrow interpretation and classification do not enliven images or artists. On the contrary, when intellectualized explanations of images are presented, the power of imagery is diminished.

If I use my imagination to go spelunking in the cave depicted in Figure 7, I become a coparticipant with the image. One image begets another, which in turn begets a third. When I become immersed in one image, I am often called upon to create another, and another, and another. I enter the cave as

Figure 7. Spelunking

would-be-master but quickly find myself in the role of collaborator. Perhaps one authentic and honorable way to interpret an image is to create another image.

A remarkable truth of imagination and creation is that they are always phenomenal; they are capable of unsettling, exciting, and shocking. Image making is often beautiful and terrifying, awful and awesome. Our familiar perspectives are torn and tattered by imagination and creativity. An artistic psychology encourages us to invite imagination back into our lives, not by changing what we see, but by how we reflect upon what we see. Every object or event that once was ordinary and mundane becomes potentially meaningful and significant. When we use our imaginations and creative abilities, commonplace objects and events remain, but they are never the same. Imagination can even change the way we see ourselves. The cavern of the psyche is a maze of interconnecting veins, subterranean rooms, dark crevices, mineshafts, air tunnels, and roughly chiseled corridors inviting exploration, reflection, and creative response.

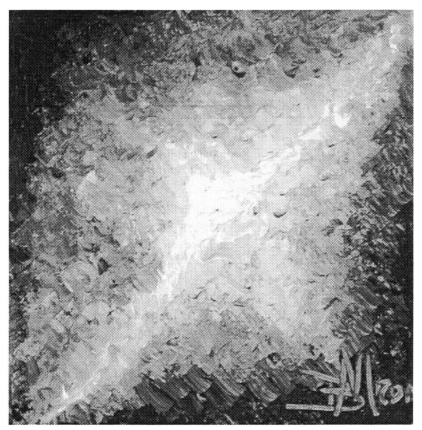

Figure 8. In order to allow imagination to re-enter life, one must learn to be still.

Chapter VI

IMAGE AND MOTIF

L ife can be so hard. Absence of meaning, boredom, and despair are often the themes that visit when one is living without actively engaging the imagination. These themes are sometimes accompanied by intense emotional turmoil and suffering. Sometimes imagination sneaks into boredom and despair through disturbing dream imagery, or perhaps through encountering a disturbing image in waking life. These images come to shock, to awaken, and to disturb, but they do not come to do harm. They come to alarm and to warn, but not to do damage. Their message is, "Get up, something is wrong, something is missing."

These disturbing internal images accompany their holders in the workplace, in their homes, and in their social lives . . . everywhere. Images dwell in the context of relationships and they long for expression. The bearers of such images long for the secure and comfortable life they have been led to expect. Employers are seldom interested in the inner lives of their workers so long as production is not affected. Husbands, wives, and others are not equipped to respond to the message of these images. Some therapists attempt to remove the discomfort brought by such images through cognitive restructuring or medication.

Artistic psychology encourages an unconventional way of

regarding the struggles of day-to-day life. It does not focus on any one symptom as being problematic or pathological. Rather, symptoms are viewed as pathos: elements in experience or in artistic representation evoking compassion or empathy. From this perspective, symptoms such as boredom, emptiness, and despair are regarded as timely messengers calling attention to the need for reclamation of the imagination, the need for restoration of soul.

Imaginal reclamation and soul restoration are processes that involve attending to the details of life's canvas, as well as to the larger movements, colors, and forms. Reclamation of imagination and soul restoration are not possible if one's attention is focused on easing discomfort or attempting to "do away with" the anguish of living. In order to allow imagination to re-enter life, one must learn to be still.

THE GATE TO DIANE

Diane, a nurse in her mid-forties, came to my private practice studio concerned that she had lost all of the excitement in her life. She complained she had no interest in her work, her relationships with her husband and children, or her crafts. She said she had fantasized having an affair with a doctor at the hospital where she worked, but even this flight of the imagination held no real thrill.

In one of the early sessions, she sat slumped in the chair across from my desk, she said, "I'm utterly bored."

"Is that why you've come to me?" I asked.

She sighed. "I don't know."

I was curious. "There are many different forms of therapy, Diane. Why not go to a psychologist or social worker, or a marriage counselor?"

"Oh, I know what they'd say. I can say all the right words to myself already."

We sat in silence for a few minutes. Diane finally sat back in the chair and asked, "Well aren't you going to do something, say something?"

"I don't know what to say, Diane. This is a mystery."

We were quiet again for a few moments. She seemed to become tense. She sat forward in her chair and pushed it back while she glared at me. "Well, this is the weirdest therapy I've ever had! You expect me to pay you for this!"

I smiled. "You seem to be livening up a bit, Diane."

"What?" she exclaimed.

"Diane, you seem pretty angry right now. You don't look bored at all. I've been trying to get some kind of a mental picture of your boredom, but nothing would come."

"This is absurd! Is that all you do, think up ways to describe your clients as pictures?"

"How do you feel, right now, Diane?"

"I, . . . (she paused) . . . I think."

I interrupted. "That's not what I asked. How do you feel?" She offered no response.

"What color do you see?"

"Black," she sneered.

"And the black feels?"

"Cold," she exclaimed.

"Good," I said. "Diane, now we've got something we can work with. You came into the studio looking empty and listless. Already we have some cold blackness."

"So what!" she exclaimed. "What does that have to do with anything?"

"I'm not sure." I said. "But it might mean that the entry point, the opening, to your interests, your passions, and energy will be a dark one. At least that's where I think we should start."

I went to the cupboard and pulled a sketchpad from the shelf. I rummaged through a box of colored pencils, and markers until I found several different shades of black. I handed Diane the pad, pencils, and markers.

"I can't draw very well."

"It sounds like you have a strong inner critic," I replied. "Diane, if we are going to work together I would ask that you try to stop saying things like that."

She looked at me suspiciously. "What do you mean?"

"You just said that you can't draw. I'm not sure I believe that. You might be able to draw anything that you want to if you'd just give yourself a chance."

"I don't understand what you mean," she said.

"Let's try this," I said. "If you could draw something, what do you imagine you might draw?"

She replied, "I'm not sure . . . maybe some kind of a fence or something, but I couldn't draw it."

"There's that critic again. I've got an idea, Diane. Show me what you imagine."

After a few moments' hesitation Diane began to draw. The image that emerged in shades of gray and black was of a wooden gate standing alone in a large field. As she worked on this drawing, she asked, "How can I make the gate look like it is three dimensional?"

I gave her a brief lesson in two-point perspective drawing. She picked up the techniques quickly. The image that emerged held a mysterious and lonely quality. It seemed to capture the wistful sense of boredom and sadness she experienced, and yet as she drew intensely she appeared neither bored nor sad. After she'd worked on the drawing for almost an hour, I said, "I have another appointment coming in a few minutes, Diane."

She looked up from the pad. "Can I take this with me?"

"Sure."

"I'll bring it back next session."

"It's a nice drawing, Diane."

"Yeah." She replied. "Where can I get some pencils and markers like these?"

"Any art store will have what you want."

"When is our next appointment?"

* * * * *

Arts processes provide opportunities to make tangible objects symbolizing feelings and thoughts that are sometimes disturbing, evasive, obscure, and mysterious. Diane's image of the gate offered us a *thing* to look at, be with, and talk about. Many people find that expressing their feelings through making images is less threatening than directly discussing emotional problems or relationship difficulties. Often people seeking art therapy have already tried to alleviate their emotional distress through traditional verbal psychotherapy without significant relief.

The act of creating an objective thing, the artwork, distinguishes artistic psychology from the psychotherapy done by traditional psychologists, social workers, psychiatrists, and other verbally oriented counselors. The painting, the sculpture, the drawing is the focal object in the therapy process. Through the creation of the artwork the relationship between artist/therapist and artist/client is constructed. The art piece provides both a subject and context for client and therapist to be together. Sometimes the artwork is talked about. Sometimes the client is asked to give the image a voice and to speak from its perspective. At other times, as was the case with Diane above, there may be little or no talking at all.

The essence of artistic psychology is found in visual images and the process of creation. Working from this perspective, the artist/therapist attends to the client by doing with them, being open to them, and honoring their pain (Moon, 1995). The primary focus of the work is involving the artist/client in a creative struggle with the ultimate concerns of human existence: freedom, isolation, purpose in life, and death.

A central tenet in therapy from an artistic psychology approach is the idea that art processes lead individuals toward a state of mindfulness. Artistic expression leads to mindfulness,

mindfulness leads to creative anxiety, which leads to creative action, which fosters expression, which deepens mindfulness. The process is circular.

Artists often have an extraordinary awareness of their own hurts. Artistic sensitivity to the brokenness of the world and the woundedness of soul is frequently the thematic focus of artworks. It is as if the artist's creative efforts are inclined toward self-healing. Old wounds from the past, traumas of the present, and worries about the future are transformed into art pieces. Sometimes the images are ugly, sometimes beautiful, sometimes courageous, and sometimes cowardly. Whether monstrous or heroic, pleasant or disturbing, sacred or profane, the arts have the ability to heal.

The creative arts were therapeutic long before the word psychotherapy was coined. The helping professions have often been referred to as the healing arts. The medical professions have only relatively recently begun to speak of themselves as medical science rather than the medical arts. To think of this book as a call to reintroduce the arts to psychology is a mistake. On the contrary, it is a call for psychology to reimagine itself as art. In many ways, artists' work throughout history has been inherently psychotherapeutic. Psychotherapists might consider entering into artistic work in order to rediscover the roots of their therapeutic endeavors as art.

Art is inherently able to heal. Indigenous peoples and primitive cultures throughout the world have recognized this truth. Medicine men, shamans, and witchdoctors have served as the catalyst/leaders of creative healing rituals. Rituals, in this sense, refer to the translation of essential myths and metaphors of a culture into symbolic actions. The healing potential of the act of expressing the truths of existence cannot be overestimated. Making art can be both a personal and communal ritual enactment that translates the core realities of artists' existences into symbolic actions (the art process) and symbolic forms (the art product).

As Reece notes in the foreword to this book, art and scientific psychology have been divorced for some time. The model of the artist therapist, immersed in the artistic healing journey of the client, is in stark contrast with the image of the neo-Freudian psychotherapist who remains opaque, detached, and removed from his client.

Artistic psychology regards psychotherapy as an art form just as surely as it regards art making as psychotherapeutic process. Creating art is a transformation of raw materials into expressive forms. Psychotherapy is a process of transforming raw potentials of human beings into meaningful whole persons.

Figure 9. Experiences are deepened, reflections honored, and imagination set apart through the actions of art making.

Chapter VII

THE ARTIST'S SOUL

Reflecting on life from the perspective of the *artist's soul* is a way of looking at the world and considering the meanings of existence in the world. The soul of the artist is a viewpoint that is contemplative and introspective. It seeks, through creative action, to grasp and express the essence of things and events. Of course, *soul* is not a trait of artists alone. However, the artist's active engagement with images promotes simultaneous reflections upon the inner and outer worlds and the feelings, thoughts, and sensations that are connected to these dual worlds. The capacity and willingness to attend to these layers of existence are what promotes the artist's distinctive involvement with soul. The artist's soul is the intersection of introspection, *extrospection,* and creative activity. It is at this intersection that meanings are found and random occurrences transformed into poignant experiences.

James Hillman (1989) discusses his concept of soul as "that unknown component which makes meaning possible, turns events into experiences, is communicated in love, and has a religious concern" (p. 21). Hillman modifies his definition of soul by adding, ". . . by 'soul' I mean the imaginative possibility in our natures, the experiencing through reflective speculation, dream, image and *fantasy*–that mode which recognizes all realities as primarily symbolic or metaphori-cal" (p. 21).

From the perspective of artistic psychology, I would add yet another characteristic of soul: *soul* is active. Experiences are deepened, reflections honored, and imagination set apart through the actions of art making. Soul restoration is not a passive phenomenon.

When the arts are considered from a *soul* viewpoint, their processes and products have the potential to be made sacred. From this perspective, artistic images cannot be regarded as pathological indicators of illness, but rather as compassionate snapshots of life. Art comes from the depths of human expe-rience—from passion, conflict, and creative turmoil.

In artistic psychology, making art is making soul. Art pro-cesses offer a new viewpoint, an imaginative portrait of the artist and the world. Painting, drawing, and sculpture create meanings and make them visible by transforming random events into ensouled experiences. There is an artistic founda-tion to human existence that is beyond language, behavior, or physiology. The exceptional gift of artists to the community is the soul/art making process.

This discussion of soul ought not to be taken as rhetoric born of any particular religious influence. As an artist, I view the work I do as a sacred pilgrimage. My mode of transporta-tion in this pilgrimage is the making of artwork. My primary modes of communication are the images I create. In the sanc-tuary of my studio, soul is made in the forms of image confes-sions, thanksgivings, and praises. It is a sacred thing to be an artist, for making art opens one to the mystery that is within one's self and others. Making art is making soul.

Art images come from the depths of human experiences. They emerge out of emotion, conflict, and creative disquiet. Art processes make meaning visible by transforming casual events into potent experiences. In the moments of our lives when aimless events are turned into meaning-filled experiences, soul is most present and most apparent. The processes of making art are processes of *ensoulment*.

Art is the visual, auditory, and kinetic language of the soul. For quite some time, clinical psychology has focused on its efforts to understand itself scientifically rather than on understanding its artistic qualities. This de-emphasis of artistic psychology has left therapists without access to vital tools needed to deal with their clients' problems. Clinical psychology is in peril of forgetting the integral connection between soul and image. Psychology has done this so thoroughly it often seems to miss the nature of the living beings who are the subject of its study.

On several occasions, I have had conversations with psychiatrist friends in which they hesitantly (and perhaps with some embarrassment) acknowledge their belief that psychotherapy is more closely related to art than science. Psychotherapy is a profoundly creative process through which the *stuff* of a person's life is molded, caressed, colored, and choreographed into a new form. Levine (1992) notes, ". . . one could speak of therapy as a creative act; the suffering individual creates a new self out of the ashes of the old" (p. 23). Monsters are tamed, victims become heroes, shadows are illuminated, and fears are embraced, thereby transforming emotional chaos to order.

From the vantage point of artistic psychology, many forms of psychotherapy may best be described as art processes, just as many art processes may be described as psychotherapeutic phenomena. When the inherent creative nature of psychotherapeutic work is acknowledged, it becomes a matter of simple logic that the arts must be involved in human restorative endeavors.

Artistic psychology defines psychotherapy as attending to the soul through creative activity. Employing meta-verbal treatment modalities, art therapists establish relationships with people who have utterly lost interest in their own inner workings. Artistic activity provides an avenue for self-expression that is desperately lacking and franticly longed-for by those who suffer existential emptiness. In an artistic psychology, the studio becomes a sacred stage upon which the artist enacts the drama of soul restoration through reclamation of imagination.

The healing powers of the arts come from the restoration of imaginative abilities. Such capacities can sometimes be nurtured in the realm of mastery of materials. This is one reason why it is essential that art therapists remain active in their chosen artistic discipline. Some argue that attention to mastery of media or process leads to constriction through specialization, and that art therapists should become creative jacks-of-all-trades. Levine suggests, "The expressive arts therapist must be at least familiar with all the major artistic modes in order to respond to the demands of the therapeutic process" (p. 5). While I embrace the spirit of Levine's words, I am concerned that being a jack-of-all-trades too often leads to mediocrity and sloppiness in the service of flexibility. I do not believe soul restoration can occur though slipshod artistic catharsis, or artistic dabbling. On the contrary, it has been my experience that such dabbling tends to accentuate existential emptiness and may lead to even more loss of soul.

CARLY'S DISTRESS

Carly came to my private practice with the complaint that she often felt "numb and depressed." She was a personable and soft-spoken woman in her late twenties. She told me she had been treated for alcoholism at a residential center for several weeks a few years earlier. She said, "I've been sober for almost a two years now and I feel pretty good about that. But I just can't shake this emptiness I feel all the time."

Carly told me she'd been going to college at night and that

she would graduate with a bachelor's degree in education in the spring. She said that she was single and "trying to get over an intense relationship" with a man whom she had thought about marrying. "He left me for another woman."

"What do you want to get out of therapy?" I asked.

"I don't know. A friend of mine suggested that I try art therapy. I read one of your books in a psychology class last year. I liked the way you talked about your clients and I've tried about everything else, so why not this?"

I asked again, "What do you want from our relationship?"

She thought for a moment. "I want to get control of myself and I hope that someday I'll be able to feel again."

I gave her a large pad of drawing paper and a box of chalk. "Carly, could you draw a portrait of how you feel right now?"

She shook her head. "I don't have the slightest idea how to begin. I haven't drawn anything in years."

"Don't worry about it, Carly. Whatever you do will be fine. I just want to get a feel for how you work. How about just filling the page with a color that represents the mood you are in most of the time?"

She looked as if she had more questions, but she began to work. Carly covered her page with gray. When she'd finished covering the page she said, "Oh, I just thought of something. Is it ok if I draw more?"

"Sure, Carly. Take as long as you need."

She drew a box, about ten inches in diameter in the lower left hand side of the page. Then, using blue chalk she filled in the box shape. In the middle of the box she added a yellow and orange flame. She gave the pad back to me, "That's all I can think of."

"It's quite a drawing, Carly."

"Thank you."

I asked, "I wonder, if the gray stuff that covers the page could speak, what do you think it would say?"

She looked at me with a puzzled expression. "I don't know what you mean. I don't understand."

I said, "Carly, try to imagine that the gray is alive. It can talk. Gray, tell me about your self."

She hesitated. "I . . . I am mist. I am cold and you can't see into me."

I thought for a moment and then asked. "Mist, what is your job in this drawing?"

Carly's gray responded, "I guess I'm supposed to keep things secret, keep it cool and numb."

I asked, "Can you see the box, Mist?"

"Oh yes, I see it."

"How would you describe the box, Mist?"

Carly replied, "It is heavy and hard and hot."

I asked, "Mist, do you like having the box inside you?"

The mist replied, "Better inside me than out where the world can see." Carly looked down at her drawing and then said, "This is a mistake. I don't think you can help me."

I was taken aback. "Carly, what are you feeling?" I could see tears forming in her eyes.

"Nothing. Nothing! I'm not feeling anything," she declared.

I sat back in my chair. "Hmm, you appeared to be feeling something." She did not reply. "Well, maybe you are right, Carly. If you don't believe I can help you, then I surely won't. It's your decision to make. Why don't you think this over? If I don't hear from you in a few days, I'll assume that you have decided against working with me."

It was interesting that as Carly left that afternoon she took her drawing with her. I was uncertain if she would contact me again. Several months later, however, she called to set up an appointment.

"When could I come to see you?"

"You've decided that you really want to work with me in art therapy?"

"Yes, that's why I called you."

"Then let's meet at the studio on Thursday evening at 8:00." I told her she might be painting and suggested that she might wear old clothes.

When Carly arrived at the studio she looked around for a few moments at the paintings that hung on the walls, the sculptures that sat on the benches and the other vestiges of clients past and present that filled the space.

She asked, "What are we going to do first?"

"I don't know," I replied, "but I was thinking that you might build a canvas."

With slightly less eagerness she said, "So, how do I start?"

I pulled an eight-foot-long 2 x 2 from the wood rack. "This is your first painting, so let's start small. I want you to measure two pieces twenty-eight inches long, and two pieces twenty-two inches long." I handed her a tape measure and carpenter's pencil.

When she had finished marking the wood, she asked, "Now what?"

We moved to the miter saw and I said, "Set the angle for 45 degrees and cut each end of your 2 x 2s." I watched as she approached the saw hesitantly. It was evident she didn't know how to position the 2 x 2, or where to put her hands so she could both operate the saw and clamp the piece of wood to the back wall of the miter box. She seemed unsure of how to adjust the angle mechanism of the saw.

I showed Carly how to change the angle and how to position the wood. I left the sawing to her. She began to pull the saw tentatively. "It won't bite." I said.

Without stopping she replied, "I've never done this before."

"You are doing fine, Carly, just fine." When the cuts were made, I gave her a piece of course sandpaper and suggested that she smooth the edges she'd just cut.

"Why? They won't show, will they?"

I responded, "No, they won't show, but they will fit together better. You'll like the joints better if they are clean and tight. There is no substitute for patience, Carly."

"This is taking a long time." She grimaced. "I thought I'd be doing something artistic tonight."

I kept working on the stretcher frame I was building and said, "Carly, you are doing something. You are learning the six Ps. *Prior Planning and Patience Provides for Positive Perfor-mance.* A lot of art making is about planning and patience."

"I've seen canvases in stores that are already stretched and painted white. Couldn't I just buy one?"

"Well, you could," I said, "but not with me."

"Why?" She wanted to know.

"If you buy a prestretched, pregessoed canvas, you're cut-ting yourself off from the process. You might as well buy a pre-painted, sofa-sized painting."

She laughed.

When each of the cuts had been sanded, I showed Carly how to clamp the two pieces together in order to nail them se-curely. After she put the last nail in, she held the rectangular frame up for inspection. She seemed proud of her work.

This session set the tone for the rest of the time I spent in Carly's life. Our interactions most often dealt with the tasks at hand, stretching canvas, planning paintings, working out technical details, and finally, framing her finished works. Each step in the process, from gathering tools and materials, through signing and displaying the completed work, was done with care and concern for quality. It is noteworthy that Carly did not come to me with a sense of herself as an artist. In fact, she brought her feelings of emptiness and despair. In her case, it was critical to engage her at the level she desperately longed for. It was necessary to help her develop a more positive re-gard for herself through doing. Mastery of tasks, coupled with self-expression, was the treatment of choice for Carly.

The heart of the therapy for Carly was doing these things

together, and taking time to invest in the quality of the work. By doing so, Carly experienced the healing effects of being in the company of another person who did not judge her or abandon her. She also received the therapeutic effects of the expressive arts processes. In addition, she developed an authentic internal view of herself as she worked with and gained mastery over materials and procedures.

A later painting she worked on during her journey illustrated this with poignance. It was a larger work, approximately 3' x 6'. The scene was of a dreary gray highway, washed in bluish light from a street lamp. The night sky was deep blue, and an old man was leaning out of an open window in a drab brick building. He was looking out into the darkness, as if waiting for something.

As she was mixing a blue for the sky, she sighed, "I hate this color."

"Why don't you change it?" I asked.

"Oh, I've already made a bunch of it. It'll do."

"That reminds me of your life." I said.

As she continued mixing ultramarine blue and black for the sky she asked, "What do you mean, Bruce? It reminds you of me."

"Well, you've told me stories about your relationships, about work and school, where the point of the story was how much remorse you have because you didn't do things more carefully, take your time and do them right."

Carly seemed irritated. "Give me an example of what you mean." Her voice had an angry edge.

I thought for a moment. "Well, how about when you were student teaching. You said you didn't really give it your best. So you got a 'C+', but you know you could have gotten an 'A' if you had really tried."

She dropped her palette knife in an incensed motion. "So what? I also told you that the teacher I was working with was a real bitch. I'll get along fine once I'm teaching for real."

"You may be right. But my point is that if you practice things in a slipshod way, then it is likely that you'll treat more important things in the same way."

"That's crap!"

"Carly, it's like when I used to coach basketball. I always told the kids to practice the way they wanted to play."

"What are you talking about?"

"Paying attention."

"So, mixing up the wrong color of paint is some big symbol of my whole life, right?"

I looked at her without speaking.

In an angry voice she went on, "You think that taking my time to mix paint will make everything better?"

I spoke softly. "No, but paying attention to the little things in your life will definitely help the big things." There was a long pause. "You've gotten into the habit of rushing through life, Carly, without focusing on anything. Is the dark blue ready? Your life deserves more care than you have given it. There is no substitute for quality."

* * * * *

Carly worked for a few weeks on the painting. She made some mistakes, got frustrated, but was able to back up, think things through, and rework the images until she was satisfied. This describes what Carly was doing intrapsychically as well, learning to struggle with attending to herself. She made some errors, became irritated, but was able to stop and gather herself, and remake her self-image. She learned to like what she saw in the canvas mirror.

I do not believe such work could have been done in verbal psychotherapy. It was essential that Carly explore herself through the experience of making art. This is not to diminish the therapeutic benefit of the relationship we developed over time. Certainly this had its curative impact as well, but our relationship was intimately connected to the creative process and mastery of materials. It was in the context of the studio that our relationship existed.

As Levine notes, "The arts are pathways or methods that take us deeper into ourselves and our experience. As we enter unreservedly into the depth of ourselves, we encounter healing energies and experience the hope of integration" (p. 23). An artistic psychology maintains a profound respect for the work, the mastery, of processes and products. All aspects of our tasks must be regarded with reverence. Images, procedures, and the quality of craftsmanship all must be embraced fully by art therapists. Mastery of materials and the techniques of handling them promote a sense of inner adequacy that is intrinsically therapeutic and attentive to the soul. Mastery of process and media is bound inextricably to self-discipline, which is likewise tied to self-regard. A sacred passion is revealed when one approaches artistic works from a perspective that values quality and expressive content equally. From this sacred passion springs a new and enriched view of life itself. Sacred passion is exposed in authentic, vital, and creative interactions between the self and the world. The artist's engagement with media and process is such an interaction.

Art making may be described as the capacity to organize raw materials and events, work imaginatively with them, and transform them into objects and meaningful experiences. Making artworks based on inner images is a process of making soul. Such work fills emptiness.

Figure 10. Imagination is a way of relating to, and expressing feelings about experiences.

Chapter VIII

IMAGINAL THOUGHT

In the early stages of the development of modern psychotherapy, human suffering and emptiness were considered to be diseases of the nervous system, that is to say, neuroses. It is interesting though, that Freud described himself as an artist by nature and a scientist only out of necessity (Papini, 1969). Yet Freud clearly focused his psychological writings on the task of forming a science of the mind. "For Freud, the therapeutic benefits of psychoanalytic practice were secondary to the establishment of a science of the mind based on causal principles" (Levine, p. 1).

As it became apparent that not all psychological disturbances could be traced to physiological roots, neurosis became a term associated with imaginary derangement. Imagination then was conceptualized as an active ally of insanity. Operating from this theoretical perspective, some psychotherapists implicitly practiced therapy that was opposed to imagination. It is mysterious indeed that one of the primary tools of psychotherapy and psychoanalysis has been Freud's method of *free association,* which is an inherently imaginative process. Thus, the principle cure of mental illness was also perceived to be its etiology. Imagination was regarded as being both cause and cure. This curious principle has its physiologic counterpart, in that the prevention for a variety of

103

physical ailments is vaccination with the virus itself. From this vantage point, imagination is regarded as both the infection and the antidote.

It is unfortunate that much psychological thought continues to regard imagination with fear and trepidation. Ideally, psychotherapists would dedicate themselves to freeing the imaginative potential of the client. No doubt there are some psychotherapists who do just that. However, it is my experience that some elements of mainstream thought in mental health still flow in the direction of suppression and containment rather than expression and liberation.

Psychology needs the arts to be rewoven into the fabric of therapeutic thought and process. The arts are anchored in the sea of imagination. Art is always an activity of the imagination. It uses actions—molding, pounding, brushing, pushing, holding, smearing, carving—to create a simultaneous vision of the external and internal worlds of the artist. Through this, the artist creates a personal metaphor, an object that illustrates one thing (life) in the terms of another for the purpose of shedding new light on the character of that which is being portrayed. The artwork holds in tension the potential for multiple interpretations.

I am devoted to the notion that imaginal (psychological) thought is extremely important. Authentic life demands contemplation. Several years ago, during a class discussion at the Harding Graduate Clinical Art Therapy Program, one of the students asked, "What difference does it make, talking about psychology in a soulful or artistic way, or talking about it in a scientific manner?" The student went on to say that in her view, "the only really important matters facing therapists today are those that deal with helping clients eliminate their dysfunctional behaviors." Her comment was a provocative and stimulating one for it began to get at the heart of an artistic psychology. Indeed, of what use is thinking imaginatively in an age that is enamored with utilitarian pragmatism and empirical research?

The current climate in the mental health community/industry has served to exacerbate the problem of focusing almost exclusively on behavior. As psychotherapists have grown increasingly dependent upon third-party payers for their livelihood, they have been subverted into the mindset of superficial treatment planning and cost containment. Imaginal thought has been replaced by technical jargon and professional formulas for success. But these are short-lived solutions that lead to a revolving-door phenomenon in many mental health facilities. Clients enter, are given an emotional bandage, and two days later are discharged. Three weeks later, they return for another bandage.

In an artistic psychology:

- Images are ways of understanding experiences and examining them from new perspectives.
- Imagination is a way of relating to, and expressing feelings about experiences.
- The word *image* connotes vivid, intimate representation and graphic, dramatic, reflective knowing.
- Images are ways of understanding by means of sensual intuiting.
- Imaginal ideas (psychological ideas) are ways of knowing, doing, being with, and reflecting upon soul.
- Images are ways of vividly and graphically representing soul.
- Alterations of one's images can change one's involvement with and concern for the soul.

For much of the past fifty years, the professional identity of art therapy has been heavily focused on the psychological and therapeutic aspects of the work. There have been many reasons for this. First, there was a desire to be regarded as "truly professional" by colleagues in other helping disciplines. Second, there was a perceived need for recognition by governmental authorities and insurance companies. Third, there was some resistance to identifying too closely with the art world.

Throughout much of our history, art therapists have worked in psychiatric treatment institutions and medical hospitals. In such facilities, the professionals whose disciplines are anchored in science–physicians, psychiatrists, and psychologists–have traditionally sat atop the pyramid of institutional power and prestige. The therapies provided by clinicians in these disciplines have historically relied upon verbal interactions with the client, psychotherapeutic techniques, and psychopharmacological intervention. In order for art therapists to be recognized as professional colleagues, and thereby assume some measure of influence and status within such institutions, it seemed necessary for them to incorporate, or assimilate, the jargon and methods of the aforementioned disciplines. Hence, many art therapists absorbed the language and values of these disciplines, and emphasized the psychological aspects of art therapy while simultaneously de-emphasizing their artistic roots. This was done in order to survive.

It is essential that we return to ideas of depth, imagination, and mystery. An idea such as *problematic behavior* may be of use to the imagination, but it is essentially an externally based notion. Authentically imaginative ideas circumnavigate within a psychic/soulful realm. They are born of imagination and cannot be graphed, codified, or charted. It is this quality of contained innerness that allows them to make meaning from the random events of the external world.

The primary ideas in an artistic psychology always involve the deep mysteries of the inner life. These ideas challenge us to reflect upon our nature and our purpose. They arise in the areas of music, art, spirituality, and in the individual rituals of daily life.

JEANI LEARNS TO FLY

The psychologist she'd been seeing in individual therapy for the past two years referred Jeani to my private practice. Dr. Jones said, "Jeani is a 38-year-old woman suffering from post-traumatic stress disorder brought on by years of physical and sexual abuse by her father. I am concerned that she has come to a plateau in her therapy. I want to get her moving again."

"Has she made significant progress in the time you've been seeing her?" I asked.

"Oh yes, Jeani has come a long way. She has a clear grasp, intellectually, of what has happened and why she feels the way she does, but she is really at an impasse right now."

"What is it that you'd like me to do?" I asked.

"I was hoping you might have her draw or paint about the things that have happened to her. Perhaps by putting these things into pictures it will stimulate other psychic movement."

(*This is a typical misconception of the purpose of art therapy. I do not believe it is my task to manipulate my clients into literalizing their past through artistic processes. Rather, I encourage clients to attend to their own inner images, whatever they may be.*)

"Well, Dr. Jones, I must tell you that I generally do not try to guide my client's artworks into any particular predetermined direction. I believe whatever needs to be expressed will be expressed."

"I suppose that will have to do. Perhaps if nothing happens your way you might consider my suggestion."

Jeani telephoned that same day to set up an appointment for later in the week. As she entered the studio, her eyes darted about and her body appeared tense. She seemed uncertain, as if she would turn and run at the slightest sign of danger.

"Jeani," I said, "I'm Bruce, welcome to the studio."

She quickly looked toward the floor and pulled her arms

tightly against herself. "Hello. I . . . I'm a little nervous about being here."

"Dr. Jones told me a little bit about what has happened in your life. I want to let you know you will be safe here."

"Oh, it's not that." She sighed.

"What do you mean?" I asked.

"It's being in an art studio. I've always wanted to be an artist, ever since I was small. But now that I'm here, well, I guess I'm worried that I won't be any good."

"Jeani, one thing I always ask of people is that they leave their art critic outside of the studio."

She smiled shyly.

I gave her a tour of the studio, showing her examples of the paintings, sculptures, masks, and drawings that other clients had made before her. I opened cupboards and drawers, showing her where the art materials were stored. She seemed to drink it all in, as if she'd been out on a desert for a long time. "So, what are you interested in doing artistically?" I asked.

"I'd really like to learn how to use watercolors, if that's alright."

"Fine, I said. "Do you have any ideas about what you want to paint?"

"Not exactly, but maybe I'd like to do clouds and sky." So began our journey into the sky. In Jeani's first painting she experimented with layering shades of blue. In later works she moved on to swirling grays together. She must have painted a hundred or more skies over the next few months. She seldom talked about much of anything other than the values of her blues, or the contrasts of certain grays. She painted.

We'd been meeting for once a week for fifty-minute sessions over the course of five or six months when Jeani came into the studio carrying a large 4' x 4' sheet of heavy watercolor paper. I said, "You're ready to work a little larger I see."

"Yes. I want to do a crystal sky with a yellow kite, and there will be dark clouds in the distance." Saying no more she arranged her materials on one of the large tables and began to work. Although she had worked consistently during all of our sessions together, there was an extra sense of intensity as Jeani created the painting.

I was working on a painting of an abstracted close-up of a face with a chaotic background. As I worked, I became aware that Jeani was crying. I turned to clean a brush; she wept silently as she painted. Huge tears ran down her cheeks and fell, splattering upon her painting. She gently blended these with her pigments, working her tears into the sky.

I turned back to my own painting, but said loud enough for her to hear, "Hard stuff, huh?"

Jeani did not take her eyes off her work. "Yes. I'm going to cut the string."

I painted for a few more minutes. "I'm not sure I understand what you mean."

She continued to work. A few minutes passed and then she replied. "I'm going to set the kite free. It has been tied too long."

Later that week I returned to my desk and found that my secretary had left a message. "Dr. Jones telephoned. Please call, A.S.A.P."

"Dr. Jones, this is Bruce Moon calling."

"Oh, I'm so glad you returned my call. I just wanted to tell you that whatever you are doing with Jeani is having a marvelous effect. So much of her past has been freed up, it's really amazing."

"Well, thank you. I haven't been sure that things were going as you had wanted."

"Why on Earth would you say that? She is doing wonderfully. Especially all of the work you have done with her about her dependence upon her sadistic father has been helpful."

"Hmmm," I said. "I really haven't done much. Jeani has just painted."

Just then I could hear another telephone ringing in

Dr. Jones's office. She offered her thanks once more and then hung up.

Within a few weeks, Jeani decided to terminate therapy with me. She assured me that she was signing up for a water-color class at the local cultural arts center. As she walked out the door after our last session together she turned back and said, "Thank you for teaching me to fly."

* * * * *

The primary ideas in an artistic psychology always take us to the deep and cloudy mysteries of the inner life. These ideas challenge us to reflect upon our nature and purpose, and they insist we mix our tears with pigment. In an artistic psychology, images help us to understand and examine our lives from new perspectives. Images offer us a way to be with things. They open us to new ways of knowing, doing, and being. Making images is a way of understanding life by means of sensual intuiting. Making art is a process of reflecting upon and restoring soul to our lives.

Figure 11. The labor of imagining and making is fundamentally an act of faith.

Chapter IX

IMAGINATION, FAITH, AND BRAVERY

Faith

The labor of imagining and making is fundamentally an act of faith. Faith rises from the soul and is made apparent in one's regard for the reality and importance of imagination.

The power of imagination and making is attested to in the Old Testament Book of Exodus. *You shall not make for yourself a graven image, or any likeness of anything that is in heaven above, or that is in the earth beneath, or that is in the water under the earth.* This admonishment captures the suspicion, fear, and awe people have held toward artists (image/soul makers) throughout history. The essence of this fear is that the image maker endangers the equilibrium societies strive to protect through the pressure to conform.

Faith in soul is conceived and born in the devotion to imagination and its currents. Its waters trickle, flow, and rush through the forms of paintings, songs, dances, stories, and poems. As attention to these currents increases, one experiences a growing certainty that there is an inner world of rich importance existing well beyond the boundaries of one's individual life.

Faith in imagination is reflected in the person who honors images and is able to consult them even in his or her darkest hours. Commitment to soul and trust in images are inextricable. Likewise, commitment to imagery and trust of soul go hand in hand. Since the language of psyche is found in images, making and working with images is immersion in soul. Images come in the forms of fantasy, dreams, and art making and contemplating. To live in a soulful way means to imagine. To be faithful to soul means to engage with inner vision. To be with soul is to be imaginary. From this perspective, psychotherapy is an act of imaginative telling of tales through creation.

Artistic psychology is built upon a foundation of making, an artfulness in line, color, form, sound, and motion. By placing the study of soul (psychology) within an artistic framework, I am suggesting that psychology can be both imaginative and creative. The psychology I am proposing assumes an artistic basis of existence. Therefore, any case illustration or case history must be an imaginative expression of this artistic existence, a creative making of poetic sound and color. From such a vantage point, truth may appear in fantasy and fact may be revealed in fiction.

To have faith in imagery is to operate from a position of devotion to imagination. As artists attend to their inner currents, they allow themselves to experience a growing certainty in inner worlds of rich importance existing well beyond the boundaries of their factual histories. The more a person attends artistically to internal images, the less likely that images will be destructively acted out on the world. No one is hurt by drawings.

Making art is a symbolic expression of hope. In an unspoken manner, engaging in creative activity is an act of generativity, a gift to the next generation. In order to do this, one must believe, at a deep level, that the next generation is worthy of the gift and that one has something of value to offer. In a conversation with Cathy Moon, she suggested that, "Such hope is grounded in the belief in art as a worthwhile activity.

To take some stuff (paint, paper, wood scraps, junk, whatever) and make something of it . . . how could you do it without hope?"

Hope is contagious and it is in the studio that faith in the art-making process is nurtured. Creating art is a declaration of faith and hope.

Imaginal Bravery

I want to suggest that making art is inextricably bound to imaginal bravery. My ideas regarding imaginal bravery have been deeply influenced by Rollo May's (1975) work, *The Courage to Create*. "In human beings courage is necessary to make *being* and *becoming* possible" (p. 13). In an artistic psychology, imaginal bravery is the courage to transform internal images into external forms.

For my purposes here, I will refer to two separate but inextricably linked notions of image: (1) a mental picture of something not actually present, and (2) a tangible or visible representation. These two are distinct but inseparable in relation to an artistic psychology. The first refers to a purely internal process within the mind of the image maker. The second refers to a visible, externalized presentation of the mental picture. The first instance may be entirely a passive experience, while the second demands active engagement on the part of the artist.

The imagination creates internal images and the artist uses these to create artworks. Bravery, as I am using the term here, is a willingness to live authentically and creatively in the face of existential emptiness and anguish. This kind of bravery implies a willingness to act creatively. May (1975) argued, "The emptiness within corresponds to an apathy without; and apathy adds up, in the long run, to cowardice." Combating existential emptiness, or loss of soul, must involve creative action as the antidote to apathy.

Imaginal bravery should not be mistaken for foolhardy

bravado. In our culture, at present, courage is too often confused with rash machismo. This pseudo-courage often leads to impulsive, self-defeating behavior.

Imaginal bravery is a prerequisite to authentic being. It is this element that distinguishes humankind from all other life forms. As May (1975) noted:

> The acorn becomes an oak by means of automatic growth; no commitment is necessary. The kitten similarly becomes a cat on the basis of instinct. . . . But a man or woman becomes fully human only by his or her choices and his or her commitment to them. (p. 14)

People define their values through the multiple choices they make in every hour of their existence. These decisions cannot be made without bravery.

Here we are brought face to face with imaginal bravery, which is the courage to transform internal images into external forms. The need for imaginal bravery is in direct correlation to the intensity of the changes an individual is undergoing. This has communal implications as well. It has always been the painter, the sculptor, the musician, the poet, the dancer, and the playwright—the artist—whose task it is to give form to the essential themes of his or her particular time. The essential story is found in the images the artist creates. In this sense, the artist engages in a dramatic enactment of the essential themes of the times.

In the latter half of the 1980s, imaginal bravery was made manifest in the images of sexual, physical, and emotional abuse created in the visual, literary, musical, and cinematic arts. The result was a new awareness of the devastating impact of abuse on the lives of human beings. Subsequently, mental healthcare providers at long last began to dialogue openly about the effects of abuse and to formulate treatment strategies to address these issues. My point here is that artists led the way in opening up national dialogue regarding abuse.

Another example is the impact artists acting out of their imaginal bravery have had on American society's regard for persons with AIDS. It was artists who reframed this issue as a medical problem rather than a moral problem. It can be argued that the AIDS Quilt did more to further understanding of the tragic devastation of AIDS than all other public education combined. As one beholds the Quilt, the cataclysm of the syndrome is simply and poignantly presented in the panels. As one becomes engrossed in the drama of the quilt, the power of moralistic exhortation fades. In these hand-made images of anguish, we see the stark summary of human loss that reaches far beyond superficial taboos and dogma. The reality that AIDS can strike anyone, regardless of social status or sexual orientation, is driven home through the artistic efforts of those who made the panels.

When we think of our creating within a universal communal context, we begin to see art making as a discipline in the service of compassion, courageous change, and justice. Making art is the human process of emulation of God, a process of bringing forth the entire cosmos. Meister Eckhart asks, "What does God do all day? He/She gives birth" (as quoted in Fox, 1991, p. 47).

An artistic psychology seeks to welcome the artist back to the center of community. "Recent Western history has denigrated the artist and created myths of alienation and isolation" (Fox, p. 34), casting the artist in the role of isolated, detached, eccentric, or insane person. An artistic psychology calls the artist back from the rift caused by the commodification and secularization of art. As Fox says, "We do not have an inkling of the power that will be unleashed when artists are welcomed back to education, to religion, to the healing arts, to the service of the people in a cosmological setting" (p. 34). The truly exciting thing about this recall is that the artists-in-all-persons are welcome. Creativity has the potential to be celebrated as an essential and basic human trait that calls us back to our beginnings, stimulating a rebirth of each individual and a restoration of soul.

Artists present life's events through images. These may be visual, kinetic, or auditory. Regardless of form, their purpose is to concretize the essence of the human experience. It is the artist in each individual that resonates with these deep and basic human themes.

If the person capable of acting with imaginal bravery is the one who gives form to the underlying currents of our day, it is only logical that the art of the present is often filled with images of emptiness and anguish. Simultaneously, there is a sense of structure in the chaos, valor in the face of senseless terror, and kindness amidst the cruelty. It is no accident that in the aftermath of the horror of the terrorist attacks on September 11, 2001, spontaneous artistic constructions (shrines) grew amidst the rubble in New York City. These artistic shrines were comprised of simple drawings, photographs, flowers, and mementos of the victims and heroes of the tragedy. "A shrine is a place that contains sacred or special objects to which we proffer attention and give value. These things carry memories and bear a significance that connects us to other people or experiences in the past or future" (McNiff, 1995, p. 60). Through their creative responses to the world, artists expose the soul of culture.

> I am a citizen of the United States of America. Our government has been overthrown. Our elected President has been exiled. Old whitemen wielding martinis and wearing dickies have occupied our nation's capital. (Michael Moore, 2001, p. 1)

So begins Michael Moore's bestseller, *Stupid White Men.* Moore is not an art therapist by profession and yet he is clearly an artist who has used his art (film making) as a socially therapeutic agent. His first movie, *Roger and Me,* (1989) documented his efforts to engage the chairman of General Motors, Roger B. Smith, in a dialogue regarding the devastation that GM plant closings had on his hometown, Flint, Michigan. He has also used his art as a means to bear witness to our times. His latest film, *Bowling for Columbine* (2002), is a painful, poignant, satirical, and enraging exploration of America's culture of fear that he traces to our love affair with guns. Although Michael Moore is not a therapist by vocation, I would suggest he is an artist/therapist at heart.

Our effort to understand the images artists present is a task that resists logical discussion. We must enter the realm of mystery and metaphor. Surely you have had the experience of driving along and suddenly being caught in the emotion of a memory brought on by a particular song on the radio. For me, when I hear The Beatles' "Strawberry Fields Forever," I am suddenly transported back in time to my sophomore year in high school. I am overcome by a bitter sweetness that is hard to explain. It has something to do with an imprecise sensation that I am no longer fifteen years old; those days are gone and they will never come again. This heightens my awareness that my life is passing away and ultimately I am going to die. The product of The Beatles' imagination transcends the temporary nature of existence. In fact, at the time of this writing, there are only two of the Beatles still living and yet their art remains powerful. "By the creative act, . . . we are able to reach beyond our own death" (May, p. 25). The Beatles' creative process demanded courage of them. So too, my active engagement with the song decades later calls upon my courage in the present. I listen, caught in a mysterious sense of awe and longing.

Why it is that imagination is so dangerous, so difficult? Why does transforming an internal image into an external form require courage? It is the anguish of life that has so often been the dwelling place of the artist. It has always been the poet, the painter, the playwright, and the musician who have been willing to risk personal safety in order to challenge the societal status quo. A clear example of this bravery was seen in the poet/song writers of the 1960s who raised the awareness and conscience of an entire generation during the Viet Nam War. A poignant illustration of this was Arlo Guthrie's biting satire, "Alice's Restaurant" (1967). The hero of Guthrie's ballad is persecuted for committing the crime of littering while at the same time being encouraged to commit genocide in the service of the government.

The primary task of psychotherapy can be described as heightening self-awareness. Nietzsche (1871) suggested the task of the artist is to present the realities of life as it is. It is understandable then that many present-day artistic productions offer images of emptiness, false conformity, senseless violence, hedonistic materialism, and exploitive use of power.

The idea of the artist as one who is able to expose the unspoken credos of an age casts the artist in a heroic light. There is a more selfish side to this form of expression, however, which is the artist's use of creativity as a means to transcend death. The ultimate existential reality is that we all will die. It is this reality that stimulates the creative person to rebel against the norms of a given time. The bravery of imagining is itself an effort to reach beyond the boundaries of human existence.

Ideas about what art is, who can make art, and who can call themselves artists have been continually challenged throughout history. In contemporary times, new genre public art or activist art is work that in both its forms and methods is process-oriented rather than product-oriented (Felshin, 1995). As a practice, activist art often takes the form of temporal interventions, such as performance or performance-based activities, media events, exhibitions, and installations. Many, though not all, of the innovators of this form of art making are women, and/or feminists (Felshin, 1995). They operate from an ethic of collaboration, community building, teamwork, mutual participation, and inclusion, thus challenging art-world notions of individual authorship, private expression, and the cult of the artist.

An example of "public art" is the work of Mierle Laderman Ukeles. Since 1970, she has worked as the unpaid artist-in-residence for New York City's Sanitation Department. Her artwork involves the community in exploring its typical indifference to garbage and disrespect of those whose work is to dispose of that garbage. In her first project as resident artist, Ukeles decided to artistically recognize the importance of sanitation work and to heal the discord between the workers and the community in a performance artwork that was both private and public. Dressed in the orange jumpsuit of a garbage collector, she walked the districts of New York and shook the hand of city trash collectors. With each handshake she said, "thank you." Out of this uncomplicated gesture a multifaceted body of exhibitions, events, and analyses grew. Such work requires bravery.

Public and activist art is rooted in the 1960s. The civil-rights movement, the Viet Nam War protest movement, and the counterculture that questioned authority, values, and institutions of the establishment all served as fodder for emergent art forms. Would AIDS still be regarded as a moral problem rather than a medical epidemic were it not for the artistry of the AIDS Quilt, which served to put a human face on this devastating disease?

Influenced by social forces and a concern for community and the world, artists have shifted their attention from making art for the sake of art, to making art for the sake of people.

In Columbus, Ohio, the Stuart Pimsler Dance and Theater Company dedicated several months to collaborate with nurses, doctors, chaplains, and other caregivers from the oncology unit at a large community hospital. Together they created a dance performance, "Still Life with Rose," that captured the passion, compassion, loss, and hurt these caregivers lived with everyday. Though not one of the performers was a professional dancer, "Still Life" was an evocative, painful, joyful, and healing event to witness.

Stuart Pimsler Dance and Theater Company has also designed and facilitated a program of workshops and performance work, *Caring for the Caregiver,* to help health care professionals express the complex emotional issues and unacknowledged stress associated with their work.

In Albequerque, New Mexico, art therapist Janis Timm-Botos was the driving force behind the creation of ArtStreet, an art studio/shelter for the homeless in Albuquerque. "ArtStreet is a group of artists, art therapists, and interested community members who want to use art to build community and increase personal self-esteem, self-sufficiency, and hope among individuals and families who are dealing with homelessness" (p. 184).

I have been interested in the activist role of the artist for many years. Although I would not have described it as such, in 1970, I was a budding young art student and objector to the Viet Nam War. I attended my first Earth Day Happening at Bowling Green State University. Over the summer, back in my hometown, I saw with new eyes the trash and litter that lined the banks of the Miami River that ran through our town. I rounded up some friends and attended a city council meeting. The Mayor and council members didn't appreciate our zeal. They saw no problem with the river. So my friends and I decided to stage an event. For several weeks we went to the river and picked up trash. We piled the trash onto the back of a flat bed truck and entered it as a float in the Fourth of July parade. We made big signs for both sides of the truck that said something like, "This is from our river. There is no problem." The city fathers were not amused. But by 1972, the river was cleaned up through a joint community effort.

* * * * *

Artists are by nature equally concerned with looking inward and looking outward. They do this simultaneously. As the artist attends to an inner vision external pressures to conform are ignored. This makes the artist a potentially coercive and dangerous figure in the eyes of the world. It can be argued that society itself is the coercive agent and the artist stands as one not malleable to communal aims. One who will not be molded is a threat to the status quo. Artists, as people willing to pay attention to their inward and outward vision, are likely to be "boat rockers." They seek the hidden structure in anarchy and expose the chaos inherent in the false order of conformity.

My art comforts me when I am in distress and afflicts me when I am too comfortable. It is the nature of art processes that they soothe and strike. Art often comes from inner turmoil, craving, and dissension.

The decade of the 1990s brought tremendous change to health care systems in the United States. I was deeply affected by some of these changes, both professionally and personally. In 1989, I was a member of a large adjunctive therapy staff at a psychiatric hospital. There were twenty-two therapists in our department. The staff consisted of art therapists, music therapists, recreation therapists, horticulture therapists, and activity therapists. As the world of health care delivery systems changed, a process of downsizing occurred, at the hospital where I worked and many other health care facilities across the nation. When I wrote the first edition of this book, in the fall of 1995, there were only two art therapists left at the hospital. I said many painful good-byes to colleagues over the five-year downsizing period. One day, as I sat with Becky Flais, who was preparing to leave the hospital staff, she asked, "How do you go on in the face of all this change?"

I responded, "I think it has something to do with ruthless determination."

She wanted to know what I meant by that.

"I have such a strong faith in the goodness of what I do as an artist and therapist. I will not let this strange, profit-driven climate dissuade me."

"But where do you find the courage?" she pressed.

I thought for a moment. "I think it's because of the studio," I said. "I have such vivid memories of the times in my life when making art has sustained and nurtured me that I refuse to let the madness of insurance companies and managed care corporations get in my way."

In a lecture to graduate art therapy students, Jim Lantz, Ph.D. said, "Insurance companies and third-party payers have attempted to make psychotherapy an accounting exercise." Jim's point was that when dealing with the inner life of another person, the product of the therapy must be thought of as awareness of what he termed, "meaning potentials," rather than superficial measurable behaviors. From an artistic psychological viewpoint, a prominent purpose of therapy is to heighten self-understanding by exposing the realities of life as it is.

Those who challenge the accepted order of the day are simultaneously anchored in their inner vision and keenly aware of the world around them. They attend to their images of the way life is, while knowing full well this may lead to rejection and condemnation. The courage to shake the status quo is found in the imaginative sounds, pictures, and words of the artist. As Phil Ochs wrote, "Call it peace or call it treason, call it love or call it reason, I ain't marchin' anymore" (Ochs, 1968).

Figure 12. Seldom does art making happen without deep psychological movements happening as well.

Chapter X

FREEDOM TO MAKE

People often come to crisis points in their lives. The factors that precipitate these are as varied as the individuals themselves. Common reactions to crises include questioning one's own motivations, feeling one's confidence shaken, and experiencing a sense of instability. It is at points of crisis that the arts processes are needed most. However, it is precisely during these periods that many people withdraw from their creativity. It is as if they believe that to engage in creative work would steal what precious energy they still possess. Whether the crisis is brought on by intense personal relationships or conflicts at work, or other individual life circumstances, my counsel is the same: go into the studio and MAKE ART.

McNiff (1989) says, ". . . our purpose [as artists] is one of awakening consciousness to the experience of soul." Seldom does art making happen without deep psychological movements happening as well. Whenever artwork is happening, there is soul-work happening, whether consciously acknowledged or not. This may account for why people in crisis are sometimes reticent toward making art.

The heroes and heroines of fairy-tales all go through times of darkness and deep isolation. This is known as the time of ashes. It is a time of descent into the underworld. Along the way, primal manifestations—a spirit, a stone, or a wild animal—help the hero. Although at times feeling utterly alone and lost, the hero/heroine eventually comes back to the light, helped only when it was most needed.

To engage with one's art and the art of others exerts a powerful inward pull toward soul. Images born during crisis periods are manifestations of soul-work in process. As a therapist working from an artistic psychology framework, I urge my clients to work with the *stuff* that is their art. I expect them to have stained hands. I advocate for them to be proud of the paint smears on their shirts. I do this in every way I know how. I am there in the time of dark isolation and descent. I carry with me a torch and a paintbrush. I share stories of my own journey. When they ask me how I survived the dangers of my dark pilgrimage, I tell them the truth. "I don't know. I suppose I painted my way to safety."

Artistic psychology hinges on the conviction that human beings have the freedom and capacity to create the meaning of their own lives. This implies that individuals have the freedom to act in whatever manner they choose, and to change when they choose to do so. In attempting to fully understand this kind of freedom, the paradigm of the artist is helpful.

Artists are constantly faced with problems that remind them they must act, they must choose, and they are free to do whatever they wish in their creative work. Artists bring all of their experiences and knowledge to the encounter with the canvas, and yet once there, must let go of past inclinations and uncertainties about the future in order to be genuinely in the present. It is essential that artists be nowhere else than in the present when creating. This may seem to be a difficult requirement, but I believe it is nearly impossible to *make* without being intensely in the here and now.

In order to understand the nature of this fierce "here and now" creative encounter, it is helpful to regard the art process itself as a metaphor. The freedom to make may best be examined through the observation of the artist in the inspirational phase of creative work. The artist loses all sense of past and future, existing only in the present moment. Totally absorbed, fascinated, and immersed in the here and now task, the artist is unfettered.

The willingness and capacity to be free in the present seems to be a fundamental attribute of creative action. This could be described as a loss of ego, or more positively as a transcendence of self. There is integration, a fusion of sorts between the artist, the media, and mythic theme. Regardless of media—paint, dance, music, or rhyme—artists say they experience a sense of ecstatic revelation, freedom, and bliss as they work.

The freedom of art making has much to offer our understanding of the creative encounter with clients.

THE ARTIST: The painter moves her brush from palette to canvas. She has done these motions before. She is aware she has painted before. She has used the same color combinations in earlier work. In this sense, her past is a part of the present. It is mingled throughout her being. Yet, she will not paint again what she painted in the past. She frees herself of the past so she can be with the canvas in the present.

THE ART THERAPIST: The artist therapist brings the memory of past encounters with other clients to the current session. Yet, the approach that was so effective with the client last week may have little or no benefit to today's client. The therapist must let go of the past in order to be in the present.

THE ARTIST: As the painter works, she cannot look too far into the future of the process. Each moment must be allowed to stand for its own sake, not as a springboard to some future process. Worrying about what comes next gets in the way of what is happening now.

THE ART THERAPIST: The therapist must attend to what the client is doing right now, rather than wondering about what might happen during the next session. In a deep sense, there is no next session, there is only this one. The therapist must be an agent for good in this moment.

THE ARTIST: She paints. She works without guile, heedless of what should, or ought, to be happening. The interplay is among the media, the image, and herself. There is a sense of childlike purity of intent. She stands naked to the process, experiencing the moment without manipulation or demand.

THE ART THERAPIST: The therapist sometimes feels foolish in the early stages of therapy. Being a therapist involves an opening of self, being vulnerable to another, which is foolishness at its best. In the therapeutic encounter, the therapist brings an innocent positive regard for the client's well-being.

THE ARTIST: Images emerge and the artist is fully focused on the canvas. She abandons her public façade, forgets her desire to influence others, to gain recognition and approval. Through the artistic process, she is able to be herself, genuinely, authentically. With no distractions she is able to attach herself completely to the task of painting.

THE ART THERAPIST: The client begins to draw. With no script to read and no theme to improvise upon, the therapist is free to be with the client and genuinely devote herself to trying to understand and respond to the client's drama.

THE ARTIST: Images continue to form. She is caught up in the birth process within her. She does not criticize or edit. She does not reject or judge the work. She just facilitates the flow of paint.

THE ART THERAPIST: As the client works, the art therapist becomes absorbed in the client's process. She watches, creates alongside, and is open to whatever comes. She does not interrupt the client or analyze. She simply lets the session flow.

THE ARTIST: She steps back from the painting to get a better look at the work in progress. She does not indulge in worrying about what others will say about her painting. She does not censor the work. In the creative moment, there is a sense of freedom, self-sufficiency, and a quality of authenticity. Fear and indecision have been replaced by inner strength and courage.

THE ART THERAPIST: The client steps back from the drawing she has made. Tears slip down her cheeks. The therapist looks at the painful image. The therapist may be dismayed by the image, but she must not fear it. For the moment, the therapist stands with the artist and they are strong and courageous together. They look at the painful image with confidence and are not intimidated.

THE ARTIST: Determined and assured, she picks up the chalk again and moves back to the paper. She accepts the image as it is. She lets it be itself. She is quiet and respectful. She allows the process to have its own way.

THE ART THERAPIST: As the client brings painful and traumatic images to the studio, revealing her life through art, the therapist makes every effort to honor these unfolding images. The therapist maintains an attitude of awe in the company of the client's artistry. She accepts the client's offerings and in every way imaginable ennobles them. Regardless of the visual form, the therapist responds by affirming the validity of the creative struggle.

THE ARTIST: She draws, trusting the process. She waits, quietly receptive. Willing to forego the desire to manipulate or control, she trusts the process.

THE ART THERAPIST: It is easier to float on water when one simply lies back without flailing about. The therapist abandons her desire to control the therapy. She trusts the process.

THE ARTIST: As she works, the bright red accidentally overlaps the dull brown. She sees the accident, and then gently, instinctually works in concert with the unexpected. She did not intend for this to happen, but her capacity to adapt to the situation at hand allows her to use the accident in a positive, nearly effortless, intuitive way.

THE ART THERAPIST: She concentrates so completely, with fascination and awe, on the task before her that she can function spontaneously. Her competencies allow her flexibility. She continually adapts to the demands of the here-and-now encounter. As the waters of an ocean adapt to the continuously shifting contours of the shore, so she is free enough to flow with the process.

* * * * *

Clients frequently say the hardest part of their artistic therapy journey is the beginning. They look at the empty canvas or blank sheet of paper and are daunted by the possibilities. So many options are open when the surface is untouched. The possibilities are endless, and one is absolutely free to do whatever one wishes to do.

All of the decisions the artist makes, beginning with the size and shape of the canvas, limit the options and bring order to the chaos. As the artist selects acrylics, she closes the door on oils, tempera, and watercolors. Through the innumerable decisions she makes, both conscious and unconscious, she gives form to the chaos of possibility.

The decisions the artist makes about size, shape, form, and media are metaphoric of the internal process of filtering thematic possibilities. Exactly how this thematic distillation happens is a mystery. It is a bit like a boiling pot of seawater. As the water boils and turns to steam, it leaves a residue of salt. The salt was always there, but it took the boiling to make it visible. The same happens within the psyche of the artist. Feelings, images, themes, conflicts, and powerful forces simmer, eventually transforming into the artist's "salt" as the artwork is completed (Moon, 1995).

Making art is an exercise in both the expression of freedom, and an expression of connection to others and the world. Whatever needs to be expressed can be expressed. Creating art is a process of constantly making choices and moving between order and disorder, spontaneity and planned composition, chaos and structure.

As the artist sits before the unmarked drawing pad, or before the uncentered clay spinning on the potter's wheel, the possibilities are endless. The decisions made bring order to the chaotic potential of the work not started. Artistic chaos calls out for process and longs for structure. Process and structure lead to product. In the world of the struggling person, emotional turmoil (chaos) also calls for process and structure. Process leads to structure and structure leads to productive and meaningful engagement in life.

BETH'S IMPRISONMENT

I worked with Beth while she was a client at an inpatient unit of a psychiatric hospital. During Beth's initial interview with the psychiatrist, she fell asleep. She was nineteen years old. She suffered serious depression. Beth's parents had abandoned her when she was two years old. Since then, she'd lived with several different sets of relatives and been in three foster homes and two residential care facilities. She'd been "on the streets" for the year of her life prior to admission to the hospital.

She told her doctor that she had no interests and no hopes for her life. The behaviors that led to her hospitalization included sexual promiscuity, substance abuse, and severe episodes of self-mutilation. Her forearms bore gruesome testimony to the despair she felt within. The treatment team struggled with how best to design a therapeutic regimen of activities and groups for Beth.

Initially, the treatment team placed Beth into a number of therapeutic groups. Among these were: Grief Group, Recreation Therapy, and Communication Skills Group. By the end of her first day, Beth had been sent back to the unit from each of these group activities. She refused to participate, swore at the therapists, and was hostile toward her peers. In the Recreation Therapy group, her explosive and hostile behaviors led to heated conflicts with her peers. In the Grief Group, she taunted others and devalued the suggestion that she might have anything in her life to mourn. In the Communications Skills activity, she picked at the scabs on her arms, and talked loudly to herself. All of these behaviors set her apart from her peers and reinforced her negative self-view.

After several days of such self-defeating encounters, I was asked to consult with Beth's treatment team. The team leader wanted to explore ways the therapeutic milieu could become more helpful to her. As I read Beth's medical chart and social history, it seemed there were consistent problematic patterns. She'd attended nine different schools while growing up but had never graduated from high school. She'd lived in many different foster homes and treatment facilities. I tried to imagine how the world must look to her. Words like chaotic, unsure, threatening, rejecting, and abandoning came to my mind. I suggested that the team reduce the number of Beth's activities and the number of staff members interacting with her. I thought Beth desperately needed the stability that consistent and predictable relationships could offer her. The team agreed to my suggestions and Beth was withdrawn from her group activities. A limited number of staff members were assigned to be her primary caregivers. I was asked to provide individual art therapy sessions on a daily basis.

Initially, Beth was resistant to meeting with me. During our first session, she sat at the table with her arms crossed over her chest, head down, pretending to ignore me. In another session, she became angry with me, threw paint, knocked over the trashcan, and pulled paper towels from the dispenser. I tried, as best I could, to view these episodes as expressive gifts that she was offering. In a sense, they were dramatic enactments of her inner experience. Her crossed arms and feigned disregard gave me a glimpse of her vulnerability and desire to escape the realities of her life. The angry outbursts presented me with a ballet, of sorts, whose theme seemed to be the rage and inner mess of her life.

As I spent more time with her, I began to get the sense that Beth had never experienced herself as having either freedom or responsibility for anything in her life. She had always been at the mercy (or lack of it) of others. As this hypothesis developed, I began to form a therapeutic plan.

On the Monday of our second week together, I met Beth at the unit. "Beth, I'd like you to go over to the Creative Arts building with me today."

She grimaced. "I can't. I'm on S.P. 2." (Special Precautions 2 was a designation signifying that Beth was unpredictable and potentially dangerous to herself and others.) "They won't let me outta their sight. I might run away ya' know." She smirked.

"I'd still like for you to come to the studio," I replied. "I'll talk to the staff about this."

It took a few minutes, but I received clearance from the director to take Beth off of the unit. As we walked out the door she turned to me and asked, "So wha' you gonna do if I take off running?"

"Now, why on earth would you do that?"

"Just to get outta this hell hole."

"I guess I couldn't blame you," I said.

"You what?" Her jaw dropped.

"I couldn't blame you for wanting to run away. Maybe if I was in your shoes I'd do the same thing, but I hope you don't. It seems like you've had enough running in your life."

It was a gray, January day. A few snowflakes drifted through the air and Beth pulled her coat tightly against her. "You didn't answer me. What would you do if I started running right this minute?"

"I'd run with you."

Several moments of silence followed. Then she asked, "You wouldn't try to tackle me or anything like that?"

"No, Beth. I wouldn't try to tackle you. You are nineteen, after all. That's old enough to make your own decisions."

"So why would you run with me?" She wanted to know.

"Well, you see, I think that you should be free to do what you want to do, and I am free to do what I want also. I want to be with you, Beth. So I'll run."

With that she began to jog. I jogged alongside her. She did not slow down until we were about twenty yards from the Creative Arts building. She panted, "I gotta quit smoking."

As we entered the studio building, I directed her to a small room, just to the left of the foyer. On the floor of the room I had laid a large square of canvas, approximately six feet in diameter. I gave Beth a gallon of gesso and said, "Let's get this thing ready to paint on."

"What do I do?" she asked.

"We have to cover the whole surface with gesso," I replied.

"Then what?"

"That will be absolutely up to you, Beth."

"What?" she asked again.

"You can do whatever you want to do on this canvas, Beth. I'll help you any way that I can, but you will have to decide what you're going to do for yourself."

"Yeah right!" she sneered. "What if I write, 'FUCK THIS PLACE' on it in big red letters."

"If that's what you choose to do, then I guess that's what you'll do. Seems like a bit of a waste of good canvas to me, but if that's what you want, I'll help."

When the gesso was dry, Beth defiantly said, "I'll need some red paint." I showed her the cabinet in the main studio area where acrylic paint is kept. She selected bottles of cadmium red medium and ivory black along with an assortment of brushes.

Beth used a charcoal pencil to sketch the outline of her slogan in huge bubble letters. She repeatedly glanced at me out of the corner of her eye, as if she was checking to see what my reaction to her graphic profanity was going to be. I did not comment on the content. I did suggest to her that the C and K needed to be more clearly delineated. "I can't really tell what it says." I told her.

"You're really going to let me do this?" she asked.

"Yes, Beth. I told you this piece of canvas is yours to do with as you wish. I probably won't ask you if I can hang it in the lobby of the Campus Center, but I won't stop you from doing what you feel you need to do."

So, Beth hesitantly began to paint the F bright red. She gave me fleeting glances, but I offered no objections. Forty-five minutes later she had painted the entire first word. As she did this, I worked on a painting of my own. My image was of an abstract face, in close-up. Behind the face was a chaotic background of intense colors. Inscribed over the colors were the names of forty-nine colleagues who had left the hospital. Some of them had gone on to other professions, some had been laid-off, and others had gone back to school.

Beth lay down her brush. I wondered if she was disappointed that I was not engaging in conflict with her about her overt profanity. She sighed, "My arm is getting tired. What's your painting about?"

I thought for a moment. "Well, Beth, I've worked here for over twenty years now. A lot has changed and I'm not always sure I like all of the changes. Anyway, I wanted to do a painting about the goodbyes I've said to people here. This is in honor of them."

She looked at her canvas and the words she was painting. "I . . . I don't mean to hurt your feelings . . . with this."

(silence)

"Beth, I know that being here is nobody's idea of a vacation. It's ok for you to be angry at the hospital and at me. But I guess I really do love this place."

"I don't love anything!"

"Nothing happens by accident, Beth. I know you must have many reasons not to love."

She picked up her brush, smeared black paint across the FUCK, then exclaimed, "Oh shit!" She threw the brush down on the canvas. "What else could I do with this?"

"Beth," I said, "you can do anything you want, absolutely anything. You know, art is like life. If you don't like the picture, back up and paint over it. If you don't like your life, back up, and start again. You can change the picture."

Saying no more, she retrieved the gesso and recovered her canvas.

What emerged in the sessions that followed was an intriguing and paradoxical portrait of despair and hope. Beth divided the canvas in half. She covered the left side with red. Then, over the red she used black, purple, and orange to write in graffiti-form the names of people and places she'd come upon in her nineteen years. She painted the right side a soft yellow-white. It seemed to glow. As the paint was drying, Beth used the wooden tip of one of her paint brushes to scratch into the wet surface this word: "HOPE."

* * * * *

If one is willing to be accountable for one's own life, that is, to be the unchallenged creator of one's meaning, then one must bear the burdens of both responsibility and freedom. At its deepest level, freedom is an expression of responsibility. To be mindful of responsibility is to be aware of the capacity to create one's story, purpose, and destiny.

Philosophers around the world have wrestled with the problem of the individual's responsibility for the character of reality. The underlying question is whether there is any objective reality at all, or nothing more than individual subjective experience. To pursue this in any depth here would be tangential. Suffice it to say, I align my own thoughts with those of Kant, Sartre, and other existentialists who express the belief that reality is subjective.

The implications of such a view of reality are profound for an artistic psychology. Let us turn to the metaphor of artwork in progress. The artist has the ultimate freedom to do anything she wishes with the piece. She must also accept total responsibility for the outcome. No one else can take the credit if the artwork is successful. No one else can take the blame if it turns out poorly. Freedom, from the perspective of an artistic psychology, is inextricably bound to responsibility. Such a view proposes that all of creation and the cosmos is fortuitous; it could have been made very differently than it was. Thus, we are not only welcomed into a world of freedom, but simultaneously constrained by it as well. There is no escaping the anguish of being aware that we are unconditionally free and responsible for whatever we do, and likewise utterly accountable for what we choose not to do.

To be mindful that we are the ones who bring into being our lives and who bring order to our worlds can be alarming. The artist accepts the burden of the chosen creative acts that constitute the artist's body of work. One who lives out of an artistic psychological foundation accepts that the world has no meaning other than the meaning the individual creates.

At every turn of history, it has been the painter, the poet, the playwright who has been willing to struggle with what is present in the world. Artists have always been willing to be wounded as they wrestle with the forces of good and evil. Artists have tolerated the pain of public criticism and censorship, and yet they have created nonetheless. There has been something inherent in artists that has kept them from bowing to pressures from external sources.

The freedom to make, I believe, is an essential aspect of artistic processes. Janson (1971) uses the metaphor of birth to describe the making of art. It is begun in an act of love, sometimes tender, sometimes pleasurable, sometimes painful, and sometimes disturbing. Birthing is arduous, joyous, and full of surprises, but mostly it is damn hard work and struggle. Making art can comfort when the artist is in pain and afflict when the artist is too comfortable. I see this time and again in my clinical work. I see clients in emotional pain create images of their psychological monsters and tame them. I watch as heroic, creative images move from within to without. I listen to my clients' stories and I hear them abandon their meaningless blaming of others and welcome courageous acceptance of responsibility for their own lives. At my best I participate in helping clients tell their stories and I act as a midwife in their birth labor. Sometimes, I become a temporary adversary with whom they do creative, healing battle. At other times, I am nothing more than an attentive member of the audience who is interested in understanding the meaning of the images that unfold before me.

Just as my clients' artistic predecessors, Picasso, Claudel, Goya, Rousseau, Munch, Kahlo, and many others, were willing and able to face the difficulties of their time, so too my clients face their demons. Sometimes clients' psychological monsters are so powerful that the drama of their lives ends unhappily. Sometimes clients triumph and we celebrate. Regardless of the outcome, I am repeatedly awed by the effort artists/clients are able to marshal.

The crucial point of this for therapists is that we can deal with the ugly and ruined parts of our clients only by knowing and accepting that these can be changed if, and only if, the client is willing to accept the responsibility that freedom to change demands. Hope can enter their lives if they are willing to create it.

Figure 13. The artist, in whatever medium, declares to the world, "I have something to say."

Chapter XI

WHEN WORDS ARE NOT ENOUGH

I am at times overwhelmed by the depth and richness of the material contained in my clients' images. There is always so much that could be said about images and never enough time to say it all. On the other hand, artistic psychology embraces the principle that often the most significant events of therapy happen in the interaction among the artist/client, media, process, and image. This speaks to a central issue in artistic psychology. How much of what we do can, or should, be put into words? The artistic psychology I am proposing in this work should not be described as a non-verbal psychology, for this defines the work via the negative. I choose instead to think of artistic psychology as being beyond words, *meta-verbal*. I believe most people keep hold of images longer than they retain words and I am convinced life's deeper moments and more meaningful experiences are sometimes nearly impossible to put into words.

We are deluged with words. They surround us. We see them on road signs, in the newspaper, in books and magazines. We hear them on the radio, on television, and in conversation. There are so many words in just one day, it is impossible to retain them all. The sheer numbers of words have rendered them barren. One can only imagine what it must have been like when the primitive human uttered a sound meaning food and was understood by another. What power, to speak the name of food and call up the image of food in the mind of another! The word was the symbol, the embodiment of the thing it represented.

Word is derived from the Greek *logos,* which refers to the governing principle of the universe as demonstrated in speech. In theology, The Word is the eternal thought of God made incarnate. When we think of words as *logos,* or as *God incarnate,* they have radically more import than is currently accorded them. The image-words of food, fire, water, or danger had much to do with the ultimate concern of primitive people, survival. Today, in American culture, all too often words disguise, euphemize, and obscure real meaning.

I am convinced the real substance of my work in artistic psychology occurs among the client, media, image, and process. Words may serve to validate the meanings of the process, but they do nothing to change the meanings themselves. In a basic sense, I believe it is possible that our most significant work takes place without speaking at all.

In the hospital, clinic setting, and community, there are many professional disciplines whose primary way of relating to the client is through verbal interaction. The special gift an artistic psychological perspective provides to the treatment of clients is the meta-verbal process of art making. I encourage therapists to regard with hesitancy their desire to talk with the client. The wish to say the "right thing" or the fear of saying the "wrong thing" may represent a distrust of the client's own inner sensibility.

Graduate students sometimes ask me, "What if I run out of things to talk about in a session?" I respond by encouraging them to trust the image. Trusting the wisdom and power of the image to be therapeutic can be quite difficult because most psychotherapeutic educational systems rely so heavily on words.

I question the need many therapists have to talk with their clients about their inner images. I believe we could do most of our work with clients and hardly talk at all. It is a reality that most mental health professions depend heavily on words to describe the therapeutic work in process. Artist therapists must function in institutions and treatment settings predominantly populated with colleagues from verbal disciplines. I believe that the best of what happens between my clients and me, and their artistic images, is beyond description. It's a lot like trying to find words to describe making love, or being hugged by my children, or watching my children compete in a sporting event. There are few words to describe such happenings in our lives.

Poems, dramas, dances, sculptures, paintings, and drawings are not mere intellectual constructs. They are glimpses of the inner life of human beings, snapshots of internal reality. Each pencil line, every dissonance, and every spot of color are announcements to the self and to the rest of humanity, *I am*. The artist, in whatever medium, declares to the world, "I have something to say." The essence of an artwork is often indescribable in words. The amalgamation of the artist as a biological, social, cultural, familial, internally and externally dynamic creator is extremely complex. The most the audience can hope to do is to catch a glimpse of the multifaceted communication of the artist. From such glimpses come the first hesitant efforts of meta-dialogue between the artist and the audience. As I look at the works of my clients, I struggle to find words that capture the spirit of their effort, the feelings, the physical exertion, and the soul of the artistic product. I approach a piece of art with a sense of reverence for the story that has been told, as mysterious as it may be. When a man scribbles images across the page with chalk, or when a girl struggles with pen in hand to find the next line of her poem, or each time a child dabs a brush in tempera and smears it across the paper, they proclaim to the world, "I am someone, I have something to say." Inwardly, they may question, "Will anyone listen? Will anyone understand?" As I approach these proclamations, I respect their sacredness and honestly seek dialogue with the images.

As an art therapist I believe that images, no matter how painful, horrific, or frightening, are not expressions of pathology and sickness, but rather of movement toward help. Art making does not create the image within the person. Art making frees the image. It brings the dark, painful, and monstrous into the light. It is survival, a celebration of life. Artists reach deep within and bring out their pain, their discomfort, and their courage. An artistic psychology does not see these as indicators of things that are wrong, but rather sees images that are transforming the self. Images are metaphors of their creator and they need to be there, just as they are and the art therapist needs to be with them, just as they are.

Images are metaphoric presentations of their creator. A metaphor is a figure of speech containing an implied comparison in which a word or a phrase ordinarily and primarily used to describe one thing is applied to another. In my work as an art therapist, this definition is insufficient for it is tied to verbal constructs. Metaphors are not only built of language, they are formed in symbolic images as well.

McNiff (1989) suggests that metaphors are images that are used for the purpose of comparison, articulation, and elucidation (McNiff, 1989). Metaphors are images. This is the key element, the most potent element of an artistic psychology. Images are metaphors containing an inherent comparison in which one thing is used to describe another. In the framework of artistic psychology, there exists a reverence for the image/metaphor. Metaphoric imagery cannot be imprisoned through vocabulary. Art therapists cultivate a sense of awe and commitment to the notion that an image can and should just be what it is. This is not to propose an anti-verbal doctrine; rather, it is a call for a strong pro-meta-verbal faith in images/metaphors. If paint is in the veins of the art therapist, metaphor is in the heart.

All things we create are partial self-portraits. Images that come through us are both themselves and a description of their creator. As an art therapist, I need to look at, and be with, the images of the client. The purpose of the image/metaphor is to illustrate, interpret, and make clear. My need or desire to put into words the essence of an image often makes me uneasy. This need seems to suggest that I do not trust the image. It is essential that those who would work from an artistic psychological foundation value the clarity of communication presented in the objects and processes of art making.

As my clients begin their art psychotherapy pilgrimage, they often feel like wanderers lost in their own private wildernesses. They ask themselves, "What is the purpose of this lostness?" For many, entering into therapy is a dramatic symbol of their brokenness. Cries are heard: "I am hopeless." "Nothing matters." "Life sucks!" Such negative self-evaluations distort the landscape in the early steps of the journey.

Consider the woman who had completed a master's degree in business administration. She was an accomplished dancer, a devoted wife, and beloved friend. Still, she assaulted herself with hostile invectives. To those around her, she gave the appearance of adequacy, wit, and achievement; yet to herself, she was vile. She found no meaning, no sense of lasting value in her accomplishments. The arts provide powerful experiences that go much further than reason. The value of art is deep and lasting because it draws directly from each individual's native potential. The development of artistic expression and ability binds the artist to all of creative human history.

THE STORY OF PAULA

She was a skittish and solemn fourteen-year-old girl. Although her parents said she was an extremely bright child, she was not doing well in school. She was socially awkward and avoided her peers. She preferred to stay at home rather than be a part of the world around her. She had a quality of delicacy that kept people at a distance. No one wanted to break her.

When Paula came to my private practice studio she made an unusual request. In a restrained and trembling voice, she said, "I'd like to learn to paint trees."

"Just trees?" I asked.

"Trees," she said.

So we began an artistic journey of mastering techniques of painting trees. We began with the basic shapes: cylinders, cones, and imperfect circles. As might be expected, Paula's timid approach to the world was represented by her inhibited use of the paint. For her first two paintings, she chose to work on 6″ x 6″ square pieces of masonite. The images were small and so lightly painted as to be nearly invisible from a distance.

After three sessions of these tight and constricted images, I introduced a new surface. I had found some large pieces of cardboard (5′ x 3′) and I taped two of these side by side to the wall. I asked her to paint the basic shapes using a three-inch-wide brush and a gallon of deep brown roofing cement. I asked that each shape be at least three feet high. She groaned, "This is going to be impossible."

"I believe you can do it, Paula." She spent the next session getting accustomed to the thick roof cement.

Near the end of that hour, she asked, "What does any of this have to do with painting trees?"

My response was, "People first learn to crawl, then walk, then run. You're learning to crawl right now."

Paula got better at painting shapes and handling the big brush. She was able to press firmly against the cardboard, unafraid that she might ruin something. The next stage of her learning related to line quality.

"This time, Paula, I want you just to paint a bunch of lines."

"You are kidding!"

"No, Paula, I'm very serious." Paula painted lines all during that session and the next. She learned to modify the thickness of the line by varying her pressure on the brush. She learned to barely touch the cardboard with her paint in order to create a thin line. She painted lines, and painted them, and painted them again. The following session I brought a four-foot piece of a limb from a maple tree and hung it from a nail above a large window. The day was bright, so the bough created a dark silhouette against the glass. The upper edges of the leaves glistened in the sunlight.

"Paula, today I want you to paint the outline of this branch." She seemed to tense up immediately and she began to work in a very tentative manner. "C'mon, Paula, this line you just painted is the same all the way around the branch. Is that how you see it?"

"What do you mean?"

"I mean, as you look at the limb, what do you see? Is the edge the same all the way around?"

"Oh, I get it . . . like the lines?"

"Yes," I said. She painted the outline of the branch again, using a very gentle, lightly painted line where the sun shimmered through the maple leaves. The other side she made dark and heavy. Light and shadow could be seen in the character of the line. I suggested she try using the tempera paints to add color to the bough.

When she finished, she beamed, "I did it, didn't I?"

"You sure did, Paula."

We moved from shapes to lines, to shading, and finally to a tree that stood outside the studio window. At each step, Paula's self-confidence grew. Her manner became less frail as she worked on these fundamental painting skills. When she moved outside and started to work on painting an image of the tree, however, she discarded all the painting techniques she had acquired. She was so concerned with making it look the way she wanted it to that she forgot to use the skills she had learned. Paula became very frustrated, threw down her brush and turned to walk back inside.

"Paula, what have you done?"

"I can't paint the tree!"

"Oh, that's the problem." I said.

"What?" she snarled.

"You said you can't paint the tree. You're not supposed to be painting the tree. You're supposed to be painting the shapes, lines, shadows, and colors, not the tree. Try it again."

Her second attempt, while still tentative and awkward, was much better than the first. Paula and I painted images of that tree many times. She painted in black and white, in roofing cement, in monochromatic shades of blue, with leaves and without. She really got to know every side of that tree. She knew it backwards, forwards, upside-down and right-side up. After a while she moved on to other trees, lonely pines, twisted oaks, and dwarfed bonsai. She would stay with a tree long enough to capture its mood and then move on. All the while she became more spontaneous in the studio, and louder and more assertive with me.

Paula's process of painting trees empowered her to move out of her delicate style. I believe that the trees metaphorically symbolized the heart of her therapy. She had entered therapy apprehensive about herself and the world. When she ended her artistic journey she was the caretaker of her own frailty. Near the end of our work together, I took H. W. Janson's *History of Art* with me to the studio. Paula thumbed through the pages, randomly pausing at a color plate or black-and-white photo. She particularly liked one of Claude Monet's paintings, *The River.* She sighed, "He paints leaves beautifully."

* * * * *

As a therapist working from an artistic psychological perspective, I believe that all things created are partial self-portraits. Every creative act is a facet of an evolving prismatic portrait of the self. As I look back at the paintings I've made and the songs I've written over the last thirty years, I glimpse the growing sum of who I am. Sometimes this is pleasant, sometimes disturbing. Some days I like what I see; some days I want to hide my eyes. Still, this is who I am.

All schools of psychological thought have at their foundations a theory regarding their practice. Fundamental to this is a perception of how the therapist may best attend to those in need. Artistic psychology is based on the belief that there is an artistic foundation to life. This foundation is built on the premise that each individual is the creator of his or her own existence. There are two essential assumptions that make up this foundation:

1. That people are free to make whatever they wish.
2. That all creations have meaning.

The Freedom to Make

In the studio, I watched as Thomas signed his painting. The image was of heavy, course ropes with a thick knot and a deep red background. Thomas sighed, "My life."

"What?" I asked.

"This is my life. Every day it seems there are more and more people tying me up in knots, putting their ropes on me, tying me down."

In this image Thomas spoke for many of his fellow human beings, as well as for himself, at that time in our history. He had no belief in his ability to choose his life's path. He did not believe he was responsible for his life. Of course, he was not free from the particulars of his life. There were cultural, sociological, and psychological facts he could not alter. But Thomas was free to choose to make whatever he would of his life. He could choose to be a victim of his circumstances, or the hero of his tale.

All of us are capable of responding not only to the world around us, but to ourselves as well. We can ponder our lives. It is the distinctive condition of humans to demonstrate both self-awareness and conscience. We can detach from our own interests and transcend the self. The fact that we can go beyond the boundaries of physical presence proves our humanity, as it allows us to forego gratification in the service to another. Our ability to disengage, to observe ourselves, is the special capacity that grants the freedom to respond to our need to make.

Artistic psychology begins with the ultimate freedom: to create whatever one wants. This freedom is chaotic in nature and often is a most difficult barrier to cross. In the creative decisions that follow, the structuring and limiting of possibility, every resolution paradoxically binds and frees.

Like Thomas, I find that as I age there are more knots and ties in my life. I sometimes experience these as confining, but more often as opportunities to more clearly define the purpose of my life, my relationships, and my personal and professional obligations. Sometimes, as I inspect an individual strand, I find it has rotted and is more an encumbrance than advantage. I may choose to disentangle myself, or I may choose to bear the burden anyway. Regardless of what I choose, I choose. These ropes are my connections to the earth, my anchor to life, but still they limit me.

The artistic therapeutic task for Thomas was one of empowerment. As the therapy unfolded, I attended to his self-defeating self-confinement. I applauded the moments when he made artistic choices. I watched him paint. I was with him as he struggled with starting a painting. This offered me a splendid opportunity to delve into his attitude toward the limits of his life in metaphor.

"Thomas, you chose deep red for your background."

"Yea, it's rather gory, isn't it?

"It looks bloody, if that's what you mean."

Thomas replied, "I guess it's just that way."
"You could have painted it green or pink or yellow."
"No," he said, "it had to be blood red."
I looked toward paint containers on the storage shelves, "I see a jar of blue."
"So, what is your point?"
"Only that you decided on red."
Thomas responded, "Like I said, it had to be that way."
"We have plenty of other colors."
"I still don't get your point."
"My point is that you chose."
"Big deal, I chose!"
By taking responsibility for his choice, Thomas began to allow the possibility of other choices into his life. In our artistic journey together, this became a recurring theme. Thomas did not need to be the victim. He was free to choose; he had the power to choose.

All Creations Have Meaning

The longing for meaning is crucial in the lives of all people. In an artistic psychology, a primary focus of the work is to accompany others as they explore and discover the meanings of their lives, as reflected in their creative work. I am not interested in giving the client clever technical interventions or interpretations. I believe that if a client does the necessary work as we toil together, she will make all the interpretations, judgments, and alterations that are important.

* * * * *

Maggie, an adolescent girl, had been coming to see me for individual expressive therapy for several weeks. She had come to me after several failed attempts at outpatient therapy and one brief hospitalization. She was suffering from a variety of self-destructive and self-defeating behaviors. Alcohol abuse, promiscuity, and a variety of self-defeating behaviors had become the norms of her existence.

During our early sessions, she was rather hostile toward me, and generally resistive and devaluing of therapy. One day, by chance, as I was walking through the hallway to the studio, I happened to look out the window just in time to see Maggie get out of her car. I watched as she bent down to kiss a little girl who was in the car. When she came into the studio I asked, "Who is the little girl?"

"My little sister," she said. This display of tenderness seemed like a spark of hope in what had been a bleak self-presentation. What a contrast to the angry young woman with whom I had been working!

When Maggie had drawn and talked about her family, she had always seemed bitter and angry toward her parents. Maggie's therapy had focused on her feelings of self-hatred and abandonment. While these were certainly issues relevant to her difficulties, the image of her brief interaction with her sister offered a different direction. It reminded me of Viktor Frankl's insistence that meaning in life can only be found in self-transcendence. At our next session, I asked Maggie to write her name at the top of the page. Then we exchanged papers.

I said, "It is so easy to forget our good qualities, what we are able to give to others. This is especially true when we are feeling bad. Today I want us to draw a gift for each other. Imagine that you have the power to give me anything you think I might need."

Maggie, who had so often been resistive and devaluing toward me, proceeded to draw an open door, with a sunrise in the distance. The emotional effect of the drawing was warm and peaceful. She said, "I feel like I've had this door slammed in your face and locked tight. I guess I want to try to let you in. I don't know why."

After I shared my drawing with her, I said, "I believe that

all things we create are a self-portrait." Maggie quietly looked at her drawing.

"That can't be. I'm defective," she said.

I replied, "Maggie, I believe you. I know there are things about you that you feel are horrible, but I see this part, too. I saw you kiss your little sister, and I've just seen the door and sunrise you gave to me."

In the sessions that followed this, little by little, Maggie became more accepting of the good aspects of her life. At the same time, she became more gentle and accepting of the ugly and broken parts of herself. Her images transformed from dark and smoldering scenes of devastation to tender and light landscapes of hope.

Maggie's last drawing was a dramatic integration of her complex inner opposites. She portrayed a villainous figure and a heroine in white standing side-by-side, hands interlocked. "I'm not sure what this means," she said. "But, I know it means something."

* * * * *

Artistic psychology is grounded in the premise that there is an artistic foundation to life. Every individual is the creator of his or her own existence, and people are free to make whatever they wish. All creations have meaning.

The yearning for meaning is central in the lives of most people. In my work as an art therapist, I have accompanied many others as they have used their creativity to explore and discover meanings in their lives. In this process of attending to the client, I seldom offer technical interventions and almost never interpret the client's artwork. As we make art together, clients make all the interpretations, judgments, and alterations that are important.

Figure 14. The journey through this book is nearly complete, a journey marked with images, metaphors, and mysteries.

EPILOGUE

In this book, I have presented ideas about soul restoration through art. I have shared stories heard from clients in the psychiatric hospital and in my private studio practice, stories that have to do with the loss of soul. Soul loss has been experienced as emptiness, disillusionment, depression, longing for meaning, and a yearning for spirituality. I have proposed that without soul, and without art, life can be formless and hollow.

Artistic psychology as discussed in this book addresses the desire for depth and meaning that many people feel and the warning signs that pester them. By making art it is possible to fill emptiness, rediscover wonder, ease depression, revive joy, create meaning, and practice a form of spiritual discipline.

I hope this book has shed new light on the complex interrelationship of art making and soul restoration. Writing is such an act of imagination, and I imagine that one of the strengths of this text is its recurrent reference to art-making processes and human compassion. It is my desire that readers will garner from this book a good feeling about the arts and psychology. I fantasize readers laying the book aside and saying, "This is a humanely written book that is ultimately concerned with depth, love, and images" (or something like that). If that happens, then I will have been successful in creating the reflection I set out to make.

Artistic psychology is a process of applying soulful artistic principles to everyday life. It is based on the notion of images as benevolent and compassionate entities. In an artistic psychology, it is impossible to establish formulas for interpretation of images or equations for analysis. In artistic psychology creative action is regarded from a perspective of pathos, a presentation of health, sympathy, and normalcy. A primary task of art is to engage people in dialogue with images about the way life is. People are capable of creative resolution of problems through artistic work. This capacity for creative problem solving can be applied to other areas of life. Healing, in an artistic psychology, is a process of soul restoration. This way of looking at the world encourages an unconventional way of regarding the struggles of day-to-day life through art processes that lead individuals toward a state of mindfulness.

The journey through this book is nearly complete, a journey marked with images, metaphors, and mysteries. I hope readers of this text have enjoyed the walk, and felt the deep joy and passion I have for the work based on an artistic psychology. I love what I do.

I have attempted to present the essence of an artistic psychology as faithfully as possible. The roots of this work lie in two worlds, the land of art, and the underworld of soul. I try always to straddle these gracefully, with care and balance. I make art, and I love. This is art and soul.

REFERENCES

Allen, P. (1995). *Art is a way of knowing.* Boston: Shambhala.

American Psychiatric Association. (1994). *Diagnostic and statistical manual of mental disorders* (4th ed.). Washington, DC: Author.

Dissanayake, E. (1988). *What is art for?* Seattle, WA: University of Washington Press.

Felshin, N. (Ed.). (1995). *But is it art?: The spirit of art as activism.* Seattle, WA: Bay Press.

Fox, M. (1991). *Creation spirituality: Liberating gifts for the peoples of the earth.* San Francisco: Harper.

Frankl, V. (1953). *Man's search for meaning: An introduction to logotherapy.* Philadelphia: Washington Square Press.

Hillman, J. (1989). *A blue fire.* New York: Harper & Row.

Janson, H.W. (1973). *History of art.* Englewood Cliffs, NJ: Prentice-Hall, and New York: Harry N. Abrams, Inc.

King, S. (1988). *Misery.* New York: Penguin.

Lacy, S. (Ed.). (1995). *Mapping the terrain: New genre public art.* Seattle, WA: Bay Press.

Levine, S. (1992). *Poiesis: The language of psychology and the speech of the soul.* Toronto: Palmerston Press.

May, R. (1975). *The courage to create.* New York: Norton.

McConeghey, H. (1986). Archetypal art therapy is cross-cultural art therapy. *Art Therapy: Journal of the American Art Therapy Association, 3,* 111–114.

McNiff, S. (1992). *Art as medicine.* Boston: Shambhala.

McNiff, S. (1995). *Earth angels: Engaging the sacred in everyday things.* Boston: Shambhala.

Moon, B. (1995). *Existential art therapy: The canvas mirror* (2nd ed.). Springfield, IL: Charles C Thomas.

Moon B. (1994). *Introduction to art therapy: Faith in the product.* Springfield, IL: Charles C Thomas.

Moore, M. (2001). *Stupid white men.* New York: Harper-Collins.

Moore, T. (1992). *Care of the soul.* New York: Harper-Collins.

Nietzsche, F. (1871). *The birth of tragedy and the case of Wagner.* (W. Kaufmann, Trans.). New York: Vintage Books. (Original work published 1967.)

Papini, G. (1934). *A Visit to Freud.* Reprinted in *Rev. Existential Psychology and Psychiatry, IX* (1969): pp. 130–134.

Paratore, P.C. (1985). *Art and design.* Englewood Cliffs, NJ: Prentice-Hall.

Pirsig, R. (1984). *Zen and the art of motorcycle maintenance: An inquiry into values.* New York: Bantam Books.

Tillich, P. (1956). *The religious situation.* Cleveland, OH: The World Publishing Company.

Timm-Bottos, J. (1995). ArtStreet: Joining Community Through Art. *Art Therapy: Journal of the American Art Therapy Association, 12* (2), 184–187.

Watkins, M. (1980). *Six approaches to art therapy.* Paper presented to the annual meeting of the New England Association of Art Therapists, Cambridge, MA.

Yalom, I. (1995). *The theory and practice of group psychotherapy* (4th ed.). New York: Basic Books.

INDEX